The Everlasting Picture Show

The story of Cinema in Clevedon & Portishead

Victor Cox. Born 1888 died 1978. Builder and proprietor of Clevedon's two Picture House's
Courtesy of H.Gough/Clevedon Mercury

The

Everlasting

Picture

Show

Maurice Thornton
2005

Published by Curzon-Clevedon Community Centre for the Arts
46 Old Church Road, Clevedon BS21 6NN

ISBN 0-9549962-0-8

Typeset by Columns Design, Ltd, Reading RG4 7DH

Printed in Great Britain by Cromwell Press, Trowbridge, Wiltshire

Contents

Author's Note

This book has been some five years in production. It has, at times, been a difficult task as much of the material gathered has been conflicting in detail and accuracy as would be expected with a subject covering just about the whole of the 20th Century. I had some valuable help from many people who are acknowledged in the appropriate section of this book.

There is one person without whom an attempt to write the book would have seemed impossible. Throughout my research Jane Lilly has been my prop and I am deeply grateful to her for all of her beaver-like work to find the unknown.

It is inevitable when writing about matters of this nature there will be omissions, inaccuracies and controversy within it. The views expressed are that of the Author. Every effort has been made to ensure the writing is accurate based upon research. Some reportage is shrouded in uncertainty and any inaccuracies found are due to material received that could not be authenticated but which was considered necessary for inclusion. There is also a very limited amount of Authors license based upon how cinemas in the periods covered would have operated.

Acknowledgements and thanks go to those who have supplied the images contained in this book. Where known the originator is listed below each image reproduced. Every effort has been made to trace owners of the images reproduced however where this has not been possible and the image is not in the Public domain please accept my apologies and efforts towards correction will be made as appropriate. It is acknowledged that some of the reproduced images are sub-standard in quality but is the best available that could be found. It is hoped that this will not impede upon the reader's interest too much.

Students, especially those who are undertaking Media studies who seek further insight into the material contained in the book may contact me through the Publisher.

Also by the Author:

Lets Go To The Pictures – A Hundred Years of Cinemas in Kettering 2000
Hooded Lion Books, Kettering. NN16   0EW ISBN 0 95370372 2 X

Preface

Nestling in its own bay in the Bristol Channel is the town and resort of Clevedon. Long past are the days when it was a busy seaside resort with Victorian strollers and bathers on its foreshore. Today it still enjoys a short holiday season with visitors and day trippers from the Bristol area some dozen miles to the North. There are still many reminders of the town's past popularity to be found, the architecture, Elton House and most important of all the Victorian pier now fully restored and a Grade 1 listed structure. All of this in stark contrast to the sprawling mass of modern housing a result of the M5 Motorway running down its eastern flank.

There is one other structure however that gives Clevedon a unique quality above the many other towns of its size in the country, notably, that it still has a cinema and not only that but the site on which it is situated has been involved with showing pictures almost continuously since 1912 thus making it almost certainly the oldest continuously operated cinema site in the country.

This book is a celebration of the exhibition of motion-picture entertainment in the town of Clevedon and the surrounding area but it is also the history of the Curzon Cinema from its early beginnings as the Picture House which has been the sole exhibitor of films throughout the years and therefore naturally features predominantly in this book. Included also is account of the little cinema at Portishead which is (it has been closed for many years) unknown to many and in danger of being totally forgotten.

The Curzon fell on bad times in the mid 90s but was 'saved' and now enjoys a respectable business life. By modern standards it is perhaps something of an anachronism. Compared to the multiplexes and film centres and many independent cinemas around the country, it is antediluvian but today the Curzon can boast of good film presentation of the latest blockbusters on a big screen with digital sound and other refinements along with DVD/video presentation and screen-talk transcription. It even has a Compton organ.

The cinema site, and the cinemas themselves, have a long history which stretches over 90 years at this time and there is every reason to believe the Curzon site will reach its Centenary, that is if Clevedon continues to support it.

This book then is not only the story of the motion-picture history of Clevedon but of this unique cinema that has withstood the threats and changes to the cinema industry through the years and STILL survives.

Maurice Thornton

Prologue

Life before the Animated Pictures

It is difficult nowadays to imagine what life was like without the entertainment we experience and have come to expect today especially when we look at Clevedon at the end of the 19th Century. The place was still a village in many ways with predominately two different geographical areas each somewhat self contained with shops, small businesses and residential occupation. On the fringe of both stood the Public Hall where the entertainment of the day took place regularly with concerts, recitals, lectures, magic lantern shows and other events. Apart from the Church Halls there would have been little else apart from the pier. There was of course seasonal entertainment on the sea front which by this time was popular with visitors and residents alike. During the summer season there were the usual beach entertainment which included Punch & Judy and Brittains Bazaar as well as bathing huts and events on the pier. There were band concerts in the Bandstand on Beach Green as well as similar events taking place in Herbert Gardens. From time to time a circus or fair would visit delighting the populace and this was a great occasion enjoyed by most.

Entertainment in the home was limited to the family's affluence. For the better off there would certainly be a piano and regular soirée might take place and family sing-songs engaged in. In those homes there would likely be an early phonograph with its waxed cylinder recordings, one of the recent wonders of the age. There would also be visits to functions at Hotels and to various social groups offering conviviality. The more affluent might also have had private magic lantern shows which were highly entertaining
when conducted by a professional operator.

For the less well-off entertainment was very limited. There were the Public Houses but they were generally not a place a family would frequent, as often as today, in fact 'entertainment' did not exist only perhaps in the more enlightened poorer families where reading aloud and similar pastimes and 'hobbies' took place. In the lesser families sewing and household chores were the norm. For all there was of course varied 'entertainment' provided by the Churches and Missions.

Travelling for entertainment was not an option for most. Although there were trains for Weston-super-Mare and Bristol travel by any other means was very limited, if they existed at all. A visit to a theatre or Music Hall or indeed the new Bioscope show in Bristol, was for the average person, out of the question.

That is not to say that for some Clevedonians the new experience of 'animated pictures' was unknown to them. Some residents may have experienced a cinematograph show or knew some one who had, but for the most the coming of moving pictures was like a new wonder of the age. It was into this way of life that the animated picture was to thrust its impact on the small country town life such as existed in Clevedon at the turn of the 20th Century.

Col. Clark's Bioscope Show with organ front 1900. *Courtesy of C. Thurston & Sons*

THE EVERLASTING PICTURE SHOW

1. Introduction

1896 saw a fog-laden March evening in London when the new wonder of the age penetrated the darkened interior of the Empire Music Hall in Leicester Square starting an engagement which was leave audiences in awe and amazement. 'Living Pictures' had arrived and there on that make-shift screen stretched across the stage the audience watched as the lights dimmed and thrown on that screen was a train roaring into a station.

So realistic it became that some started to run for the exits but then the scene changed to workers leaving a factory and a boy playing with a hose-pipe and other magical images appeared thrilling the crowd spellbound by the spectacle they were witnessing .

The beginning of cinema in Britain was born at that famous London Music Hall on that night, just two weeks before the same phenomenon had been demonstrated at the nearby Regent Street Polytechnic. The audiences experienced a vision of utter disbelief such as their eyes had never witnessed before. Little wonder that they did not understand it at first. Suddenly right before their eyes were images of people scurrying about brought to life through that magic beam in a way that was incomprehensible to them.

The images might only last for a few seconds, or perhaps a minute at most, but the jerky and dim lit pictures captured audiences so much so that the show was to continue at the Empire for fourteen months to packed houses with programmes of mixed favourites from the Lumiere Brothers and varied and topical programmes made by British cinematographers.

'Living Pictures', as they were then called, spread rapidly throughout the country. First to Brighton, then Newcastle, Blackpool, Manchester and other places until by December of that year they were a success in well over seventy cities and towns around the country.

By the early 1900s Bioscopes had appeared throughout the country and films were being shown in halls, theatres, on fairgrounds and in circuses and were the way in which the majority of the population saw the films. Big touring companies, such as W.C. Poole's 'Myoriama',

Showman's engine hauling a Animated Picture show 1902. *C. Thurston*

La Sortie des ouvriers de l'usine Lumière (Lumières, 1895).

L'Arroseur arrosée (Lumières,

The Lumiere Cinematographe and scenes from two of the first films. *Authors collection*

would supplement their historical and topical stage tableaux with film using the Bioscope. Every showman worth his salt hauled a Bioscope Show.

Showmen such as Dooners, Hancocks, Thurston's and Taylors, to name a few, were touring a Bioscope show around the country by 1900. The fairground Bioscope was a two-wagon front side-show. Inside they were lavishly appointed, the front rows nothing more than benches but the ones further back well upholstered. At one end was a stage with a screen suitably arranged. At the other end was, to many, a strange looking machine not unlike a magic lantern with the operator turning a handle driving the short film through the mechanism and by the use of a light source, either oil, gas or by limelight, 'throwing' flickering pictures on to the screen.

Most Bioscopes would have an organ front with a mammoth fairground organ, a Merenghi, a Gavioli or a Chiappa, and a stage area in front of it for the dancing troupe and the barker. Power was provided by a magnificent showmen's steam engine, usually a Burrell, which was also used to haul the Bioscope from place to place, providing all the power needed for much of the fair . It was this way that many towns and villages were first introduced to moving pictures. It is known that Taylor's show was one of the first to adapt a side show into a Bioscope and toured in the summer season of 1897. For just 2d.you could see the 'latest pictures' and often showmen would film local scenes in advance to show on their visits. Most often dancing troupes and entertainers would accompany the Bioscope. The first appearance of cine-variety perhaps? but it also began the long association of cinemas with organs.

In those early years of the last Century the fairground Bioscope would have been the way that pictures came to local towns and villages. Until around 1909 there were no fixed cinema sites and there were only two forms of film showmanship those being the Music Halls and travelling exhibitors including the fairground Bioscopes.

Treading in the footsteps of past magic lantern lecturers came the Bioscope exhibitors hiring large public halls for engagements of longer film shows than usually found playing on the Music Hall bills.

In the final years of the Edwardian era however cinemas were being built for the purpose of showing pictures and halls and theatres were being converted to exhibit films which saw the quite rapid demise of the travelling Bioscopes on fairgrounds and elsewhere as showmen diversified by building or converting halls as cinemas benefiting from all-year around business. Legislation was also brought in with the Cinematograph Act of 1909 to counter the number of serious incidents being experienced and to regulate the new industry especially to prevent incidents such as fire and injury in Bioscopes. Cinemas were now becoming big business.

The first known commercial Cinematograph show in Bristol was for two weeks in 1896 at the Tivoli Music Hall in Broad Street but it was to be 1908 before Bristol was to see its first permanent cinema, the Bio, which was set up in Counterslip Hall close to Courage's Brewery, itself now but a memory .

An early hand-turned projector likely used in travelling Bioscope shows. *Authors collection*

In Weston-super-Mare the first permanent cinema is thought to have been the Electric Theatre, perhaps 1909, though there is little written about it other than it was situated somewhere in the vicinity of where the Winter Gardens are today.

As for Clevedon . . . well there begins our story.

2. Showmen and Entrepreneurs

So when did 'animated pictures' come to Clevedon and start over ninety years of cinema entertainment of which the town can lay claim? The answer is not at all straight forward. The popular belief is the Cox family were responsible but both James Newton Cox and his son Victor did not come on to the scene it seems with the showing of motion pictures regularly to the general public until towards the end of the first decade.

Although there is no recorded occasion of either a fair or a circus bringing a Bioscope to Clevedon Lord Sangers Circus did visit Clevedon and tented in Parnell Road. It ran for three days from 23 July 1910 and probably there was a Bioscope Show attached to the circus. There is also record of local Bioscope shows in Herbert Gardens which were presented by the then established Clevedon Cinephone, Company (J.N. Cox, his son Victor and others) which were very popular. There were of course the touring Bioscopes of which there were many but they would have to have been assured of good returns for a visit so it was unlikely they would have toured small communities. So it was left to 'local' interests to bring the 'animated pictures' to Clevedon.

To mark the beginning of 'cinema' in Clevedon it is necessary to take the first recorded public show as the criteria. This would not be so for the surrounding area however because there is a record of a Mr R.G. Law giving a cinematograph show of animated photographs on a Friday in October 1903 which included scenes of the Boer War as well as comedy with the screening of 'The Miller & the Sweep' (1902) and other subjects, in the old Tickenham Village Hall.

One of the first public affairs with the moving picture in Clevedon seems to be a show arranged by Mr Britten in the Public Hall, Albert Road which is now the site of the Clevedon 'Mercury' Publishing Company offices. The show took place on Thursday evening 6 March 1902. William Britten lived in Highdale Road, Clevedon and had a business in Hill Road known as the Clevedon Bazaar selling glass and china and other wares, many for hotel and restaurant proprietors, dealers, brokers etc. and apparently a library of books. He later moved to premises opposite the pier and transferred the library books there also. The advertisement opposite appeared in the 'Mercury' dated 1 March 1902. and is reproduced.

The result was seemingly successful because a number of repeats apparently took place of a similar nature organised by Mr Britten. A technical description of the Photo-Projectorscope is given in the technical detail at the end of this Chapter.

A TREAT FOR JUVENILES

*

Mr Wm. Britten begs to announce that he has made arrangements with
Messrs. HUSBAND & SONS of BRISTOL
To give an exhibition in the PUBLIC HALL, CLEVEDON
On THURSDAY MARCH 6.
At 6 o'clock in the evening
on their new

PHOTO-PROJECTORSCOPE

For reproducing Animated Photographs being remarkably clear and a
improvement on the Cinematograph. The pictures will include

*

Military – National – Patriotic – Topical – Comic etc.

*

Vocal and Instrumental music under the direction of Mr Somerton

*

Tickets will be given away at BRITTENS BAZZAR opposite the PIER
on the following conditions.

To the purchaser of the value of 6d … One Front Seat Ticket
To the purchaser of the value of 3p… One Second Seat Ticket
Adults in Charge Front Seats 6d. Second Seats 3d.
Early application is necessary as the number will be limited.

The next reference to public shows of motion pictures brings us to the family who
are most noted for the development of cinema in Clevedon – James Newton Cox
and his son Victor.

James Newton Cox was born in 1851, Living in Clevedon and employed as a
stonemason he married his first wife, Johanna in May 1879. Johanna died in
August 1881. There was a child, a daughter Catherine, but she died in January
1882. James married again, this time to Maria Anna, and they had a son, Victor.
He was born in 1887 at which time James Newton Cox was described as a
Sculptor. Victor's mother died soon after he was born.

James Newton Cox was to re-marry again, this time to Blanche Harwood who
became, of course, Victor's stepmother. She was a lady of the Arts who travelled the
stages of Europe and was an accomplished diva. A gracious lady, her performances
were toasted by her admirers with champagne drank from satin slippers. She was to
become very close to Victor and stayed with him until her death.

By the early years of the 20 Century James Newton Cox had become a respectable businessman, running a stone and monumental mason establishment which eventually became J.N. Cox & Son. By that time the fledgling motion-picture business had become a challenge to those whom had a flair for it and cameras, as well as projection machines, were readily available to those who could afford them. It is known that both James Newton Cox and Victor had such interests and that these were to blossom into vision and enterprise.

Victor was educated at Clevedon College and was an academic. He had an artistic talent and by the turn of the Century was at the school of Woodcarving at

South Kensington, London from which he attained prowess in clay modelling, anatomy and drawing. Victor was an accomplished pianist and whilst in London he became fascinated with the burgeoning moving picture phenomenon. On his return to Clevedon he joined his fathers Mason's business.

At this point clarity seems to become obscure. It is generally accepted that Victor Cox on a visit to Paris came upon a small hand-cranked film projector and brought it back to Clevedon. Unfortunately there is no authenticity attached to this legend and one wonders whilst he was fascinated by motion pictures it took the trip to Paris to obtain one when there were excellent machines manufactured in England, notably Brighton, by that time which he could have purchased however, we will proceed with the legendary account.

Here again there is some conjecture because it is known that public exhibitions were given from time to time in Clevedon by Victor Cox and others. However, by late 1910 both James Newton Cox and Victor perceived that as well as having a very interesting sideline there was also money to be made in showing moving pictures as they were a type of entertainment that had caught on in a big way up and down the country. In fact by this time of course purpose-built cinemas were being established in profusion.

One show given in Herbert Gardens took place in November 1911 by the Clevedon Cinephone Co. described as a Bioscope show, and included the Coronation of King George V and the Naval Review amongst many other items. The show ended at 11 pm Legend has it that the Coronation film was not shown on that occasion as it did not arrive from London in time.

The Clevedon Cinephone Company was formed specifically to exhibit motion-pictures which had as its proprietors James Newton and Victor Cox and an associate Mr Kirkpatrick. It traded at 100 Old Church Road, Clevedon.

Kirkpatrick senior started work as an Ironmongers assistant but by 1910 was a respected businessman in Alexander Road trading as an Ironmonger and cycle shop He had three sons Henry, the eldest, Fredrick and Edwin who was the youngest and the nearest in age to Victor Cox. At the first public shows Mr Fitzpatrick was billed as the projectionist and that could have been any one of those as no first name initial appears in the records although all of the family may have been involved given their father's mechanical background.

The start of regular picture shows took place in October 1910. Operated by the Clevedon Cinephone Company and run in the Public Hall. The first show took place on Thursday, October 22, a dark and unfriendly night. The projectionist was Kirkpatrick and music to accompany the films was provided by Victor Cox at the piano. The publicity advertising the show was headed 'ANIMATED PICTURES' with the main attraction 'Revolution In Portugal' and a supporting programme of 'living pictures' of various lengths and subjects.

To all accounts the show was a resounding success. The Public Hall was well filled and for some of that first audience, a memorable experience. Whilst cinema was well established by this time in Bristol the average Clevedonian rarely or if ever travelled to the City for entertainment. Public transport was sparse except by train via Yatton. One can then imagine the excitement that was building up in the Public Hall that night minutes before Mr Kirkpatrick struck the lamp on the projector in the dimmed hall and the first images were thrown on to the screen with Victor Cox accompanying on the piano.

Scenes were played on the screen showing the dreadful War in Portugal. Many sitting there watching the bloody fighting in life-like proportions had difficulty in coming to terms with it and one wonders whether it was perhaps the right film to begin the enterprise, but others were fascinated. The remainder of the programme more than made up for the main attraction with comedy and interest reels.

One week later Clevedon Cinephone advertised another show at the Public Hall this time the programme was advertised as

> 'Kidnapped Servants'
> 'Knights In Armour'
> 'Persuasive Powers of a Revolver'
> 'Salt Harvest'
> 'King Cotton'

I can find no details about these titles and whilst the programme looks impressive by its length most films were only one-reelers, about ten minutes, so with intervals of music and perhaps a song or two from a local artiste the show would be barely ninety minutes. This programme was more popular than the first and had to be repeated the following Tuesday and Wednesday evenings. On this occasion the pianist was a Mr C.T. Grenfield of Weston-super-Mare.

Another show of note in the Public Hall was the Delhi Durbar Celebrations which had been filmed in 1903 and was eventually shown to Clevedon audiences on 17 and 18 January 1912. Another public show of note in the Public Hall took place on 11 October 1912 at 8 pm when included in the programme was the Lord Mayor of London's Show. This date was likely the first children's show in Clevedon, not withstanding the one organised by Mr Britten in 1902. The programme included 'Fairytale', 'Casilda' and other titles. It started at 5.30 pm and the admission was 2d.

It is perhaps important to briefly describe the films of this era (bearing in mind that by this time they were already quite old) Narrative films (one that tells a story) were only in their infancy, the first was made in 1903. Films were rarely over 1000 ft in length, most much shorter, and ran between eight to ten minutes depending on speed they had been filmed and were projected at what speed the operator turned the handle. They were almost invariably 'actualities' with as yet no notion that the camera could be used to tell a story.

'Revolution In Portugal' was almost certainly an *actualites reconstitutee* a sort of newsreel. 'Kidnapped Servants' etc. were likely British reels with a hint of story but mostly portraying incidents or themes. The move to Hollywood by American film makers had, since 1907 grown rapidly many famous film companies already being established but their product had either not reached Europe or buying and renting costs were high. The films shown by the Cox's probably came from Britain's premier producer of the time, Charles Urban. This was probably the reason why familiar titles that we recognise today did not appear to have been shown. That trend of home-spun booking was to proliferate throughout Clevedon's cinema history. This being the case what was shown was obviously well received.

So cinema became well established in Clevedon. Clevedon Cinephone Company advertised weekly shows when the Public Hall was available.

The time was ripe for further development.

Technical

1902   PHOTO-PROJECTOSCOPE
Reported used for the shows put on by Britten and provided by Husbands Photographic Ltd. of Bristol. The Projectorscope can be traced to Thomas Edison who apparently designed this instrument along with many others. It was essentially a development from experiments by Edison and his young laboratory assistant William Kennedy Laurie Dickson. Edison marketed a number of projection machines in association with others inventors notably Thomas Armatt. The Projectorscope is patented as of 1897.

1910   The projector used by the Clevedon Cinephone Co. at that time was a WRENCH. These projectors were manufactured by John Wrench and Sons of the Grays Inn Road area of London in association with a Henry Joy. Wrench were in the business primarily to work on a colour film system called KINECHROME, which was very similar to Kinemacolour. They manufactured the Wrench projector for use as a Bioscope the machine having been put together by Hepworth, Moy and Darling who were all well-known names in the 'motion picture' business at that time.

It is also known that Wrench had a hand in making Robert W. Paul's (1869–1943) 'Theatrograph' projector (later known as the Animatograph). He was exhibiting British made moving pictures at the London Alhambra Theatre of Varieties with the machine at the same time as the Lumiere's Empire, Leicester Square performances in 1896 with their Cinematographie.

The WRENCH was certainly the projector used in the Public Hall shows and the Bioscope shows put on by the Cinephone Co. It almost certainly was the first projector used in the Picture House of 1912.

A WRENCH 35mm silent projector. One such as this was used to show 'living pictures' in the Public Hall from 1910 to early 1912. It is probable that a Wrench projector was used for a short time in the new Picture House. The lamphouse would suggest either oil lamp, limelight or even gas illumination.
Courtesy of Alan Smart

3. The First Picture House

There have been two distinct cinema buildings in Clevedon. The first was built in 1911/12 and the second (the present Curzon building) between 1920 and 1922.

Looking at the map of the area of Old Church Road, Clevedon in 1903 it shows that there was land between Lower Queens Road westward to where the Land Yeo met Old Church Road near to Hillside Road. Within this parcel of land stood a beer house, a coal yard and later a Police Station. There was a small roadway which led to a bridge over the Land Yeo then to a footpath. Westwards along Old Church Road up to where the river met the road consisted of two pieces of land , both owned by Sir E. Elton.

In 1903 Albert Type, who lived in Coly House, 39 Old Church Road (now the Dental Surgery) submitted plans for stables and a coach house for his horse-drawn taxi (Flys) business having purchased the land in 1900 from Elton. These were duly built and the remains can be seen today at the rear of the cinema on Great Western Road, the lower section nowadays being a warehouse and the upper the home of Curzon FM the local Community Radio Station.

Next to Type's land was a plot rented by J.N. Cox, stonemason which was used as part of his masonry yard and for workshops. It was an odd shaped piece of land which was square to Old Church Road and Type's land running back to the Land Yeo but on the west side curved to the bank of the river. It was on this piece of land the Cinephone Company, headed by John Newton Cox and Victor Cox, put up plans for the first cinema.

The first Picture House circa 1912. *Courtesy of David Long*

The first Picture House. This picture would seem to be the enlarges cinema as there is a distinct rise in the roof level away from the front of the building. This was not the case with the 1912 cinema – the change being made in 1913. The occasion for the flag decoration is not known but probably to mark the re-opening in 1913. *Courtesy of Clevedon Mercury*

Work started in the Winter of 1911 to the design by Victor Cox, who had put up most of the capital needed and by April 1912 the building was completed. Only one record seems to exist in planning form and that was for an engine house at the rear of the cinema.

The cinema opened in April 1912 details of which I will describe later. It was quite an attractive building and despite much scepticism by the population was to become a resounding success.

A sketch of the first Picture House in Old Church Road around 1912. The drawing was made by artist S. Loxton and reproduced by courtesy of the Loxton Collection and Bristol City Council Library Service.

The PICTURE HOUSE, Old Church Road.

7 to 10, CONTINUOUS PERFORMANCE EACH EVENING.

Matinees on Wednesdays and Saturdays at 3.

An Entertainment that pleases Old and Young.

Front elevation of the first Picture House. The entrance doors are those now in preservation at the Curzon. The picture, taken for publicity shows the two Commissionaires employed at that time. The photograph comes from the Christmas supplement published by The 'Mercury' newspaper issued 14 December 1912. *Courtesy of Clevedon Mercury*

It was a single story building in the Wren style with seemingly a flat roof extending back, and was constructed in brick, iron and concrete with a small sloping roof extension on the rear, ostensibly the engine house. The front on Old Church Road was of dark red brick designed in the Ionic style with a timber cornice. It was supported by six ornate Ionic timber pillars rising from an abutment adorned with denticles. Below this the entrances had similar pillars each side which supporting the pediment. All the timber-work was painted in white. The building was 24 ft high on the front (Old Church Road end) sloping backwards to 18 ft at the rear.

The entrance doors were panelled with mirrored Japanese glass. The front was bedecked with numerous flowered hanging baskets and display boards were set between the two entrances. THE PICTURE HOVSE was monumentally inscribed in Roman lettering on the pediment with a decorative finial atop the gable apex.

Internally the cinema hall was forty feet long and twenty-seven feet wide. It had 200 open backed comfortable tip-up seats upholstered in red leather the first few rows in the front were benches. The screen was an adequate 12 ft x 12 ft which was fitted on the Old Church Road end of the hall between and above the to side entrance doors from the street and pay box. Below the screen was an orchestra pit with an upright piano upon which stood a gramophone with a large horn which was used to accompany films or provide interval music. The interior lighting was by gas with some electric lighting. A 6.5 gas engine was installed at the rear of the building and electricity was provided in the cinema for projection and lighting. Ventilation was achieved by two intake grilles eight foot from the floor the air then being extracted by an electric fan. An 'ozoniser' spray was used after each performance. Gas was also used for secondary lighting.

The interior décor was predominantly maroon. The pilasters were painted white and the screen had a gold surround. The projection room was at the far end constructed in iron and brick and was completely isolated from the seating. Work to build the cinema took a little over two months and was ready for use in early April 1912.

A report in the local paper of 6 April claimed the new cinema had excellent seating, sloping floor, perfect ventilation, flickerless pictures and would have up-to-date subjects all at popular prices and an announcement that the new Picture House would open the following week..

The Picture House was due to open on Monday, 15 April 1912 at 7 pm but this was cancelled due to the licence not being satisfactorily awarded and I suspect because of tragic occurrence that had taken place during the previous night.

The Wednesday before the most wonderful ship ever to grace the seas of that age sailed from Southampton to begin her maiden voyage to New York via Cherborg and Queenstown. The tragedy enacted on the night of 14/15 of April needs no further relating here but by the end of that fateful Monday the disaster left the Nation in deep shock and mourning for over 1500 souls who were lost at sea. Whilst the loss of RMS 'Titanic' was not the prime cause of the failure to open the little cinema it surely would not have been prudent to celebrate the opening of the cinema at that time and therefore Saturday 20. April was finally chosen as the day for the opening to take place.

Handbill for the special afternoon show in aid of the Lord Mayor of London Appeal for the families of the RMS 'Titanic' victims. This is regarded as the first public show in the new cinema. *Courtesy of S. Drew*

Handbill for the Grand Opening of the first Picture House on the evening of 20 April 1912 at 7 pm. *Authors collection*

The Grand opening took place at 7.00 pm with a full programme of films which included:

> 'Child Cuckoos' adapted from the novel 'Blue Lagoon'
> 'Mary's Strategem'
> 'Dalls Girls'
> 'My Sweetheart'
> 'Fighting Blood'
> and a selection of amusing shorts
> The Gaumont Graphic, a newsreel of the day, issued on 17 April included items: The Titanic sailing, South London Harriers Race Meeting at the Oval, Unveiling of a monument to the late King Edward VII at Cannes, Shop Acts protest meeting in Trafalgar Square and more items about the loss of the Titanic.

The prices of admission were 3d., 6d. and reserved 1/-.

The little cinema was packed to capacity that balmy April night with many turned away and those with the wherewithal to afford the price of a reserved seat having booked them solid days before.

This Grand opening was somewhat upstaged however by a special showing at 3 pm that afternoon. The Lord Mayor of London had raised a Fund for the relief of the families who had lost their lives in the Titanic and the cinema trade had responded with encouragement to cinema owners to run appeals in their houses. Victor Cox opened the Picture House that afternoon for a special showing of films concerned with the tragedy. The prices for this matinee were 2/- and 1/-. The show consisted of part of the evening performance, mainly the 'newsreels' and a special film which had been rushed out which used footage of the 'Titanic's' sister ship 'Olympia' and closed with a very moving Epilogue. This film was shown at the Curzon in April 1997 and in fact is claimed to be the one shown at that very afternoon in the new Picture House.

The new Picture House was immensely popular and the need to expand after a year of operation critical. By 1913 performances were running continuously from 7 pm until 10 pm every weekday with matinees every Tuesday and Saturday. Plans were submitted to enlarge the cinema. It closed on 31 May 1913 for alterations. The last films to show in the original cinema were 'The Panthers Prey' (1909) and 'The Pirates Daughter' (1911).

Work commenced on 1 June Major improvements included enlarging the auditorium, improving ventilation by installing a sliding roof, an increase in seating from the existing 200 to 349, two more exits added and a complete redecoration and up-dated lighting. A picture shows that the enlargement

Interior of the first Picture House after the enlargement in 1913 (seen on both sides of the picture). The phonograph below the screen is said to have stood on the piano which suggests that there was a small orchestra pit as the piano cannot be seen. *Courtesy of Clevedon Mercury*

auditorium was to both sides of the building which was achieved utilising some spare land before Alfred Type's boundary or perhaps an 'agreement' between the Cox's and Type and that rented by Cox to the west boundary.

The auditorium was now 72 ft long and 40 ft at its widest point. The roof slant was reversed and was now 33 ft high at the rear wall. The interior décor was tasteful with red up to the dado and above that cream crested wallpaper. The frieze was pink which toned down to white. The interior pilasters were white with dark grey bases and were decorated with swags of imitation flowers, hand painted in oils, and cherubs were introduced at the crests. The screen was surrounded with red lighting.

The ceiling was done out in oak and a sliding roof was introduced for further ventilation and two extraction fans were installed.

A new gas engine with the capability of 12.7hp was installed as were two new projectors. The cinema was now completely electric, inside and out, and it is said that it was the first public building in Clevedon to completely use the new energy of the time. It was all completed by 14 July Contrary to legend there were no cinema programmes between 31 May and 13 July. The extended cinema re-opened on 14 July with 'Lorna Doone' (1912) and 'Father' (1909)

A report of the time tells of the marvellous experience of going to the little cinema especially when its sliding roof was open and the summer stars added to the fantasy world being played out on the screen. The tinkle of the piano and the evening scents on the breeze made for a serene evening out and when in the winter the roof was closed tight it was cosy and dreamlike inside. Nothing is said of what happened when a sudden shower would descend on Clevedon and the roof was open however, the little cinema was to meet the needs of the Clevedon public until the end of the second decade.

Shortly after its re-opening the first great tragedy of the 20 Century was being acted out and the cinema was showing on its screen the suffering and progress of the First World War. Not since the first picture shows in 1910 were Clevedon audiences to witness the actualities of war depicted in such vivid and perhaps exciting images. There were army camps on the fringes and in the town and their occupants would swell the cinemas nightly attendance with extra shows being provided to accommodate the patronage. One of the regiments stationed locally was the East Lancashires and they were to see themselves on the Picture House screen on occasions.

Interesting to note, and a point which is made many times in this book, is the predominance of British film shown at the Picture House. In this period of time films from the USA were expensive. Hollywood was still developing. British films had not passed beyond the stage of being 'photographed stage productions' and the 'star' had not emerged. British actresses were unable to emote, it took an American actress Florence Turner to change that, and leading men were subjugated to wooden performances. Low pay and ignorance played a part too. One film maker of the day, Cecil Hepworth is said to have seen no difference between an actor or an electrician.

It was to fall to British actors such as Percy Morgan, Betty Balfour, Henry Edwards and Chrissie White to become popular with the public. Donald Calthrop and Frank Stanmore, as exceptional character actors, entertained the Picture House audiences with delight. That the little cinema did so well must also be put down to the fact that moving pictures were still a modern marvel to the majority of audiences.

In 1915 a certain lad was about to start his long career at the Picture House. He was Stanley Newton and we shall read more about him later. The pay for the projectionist in 1912 was £1. 5s. 0d. per week and it was still thought to be Mr Fitzpatrick.

By 1919 however, with business still brisk and developments in the cinema industry striding ahead time for further expansion had arrived and Picture House 2 was firmly in the minds of the Cinephone Company.

Technical

No authentic records exist as to what the projection equipment was at the opening of the cinema in 1912 but some speculation may help.

It was likely that the WRENCH, which had been giving superb service in different locations prior to the opening was to find use in the new cinema before being pensioned off with the replacement of a single hand-cranked GAUMONT CHRONO. A new source of energy, electricity via the gas engine, was brought into use.

With the opening of the extended cinema in 1913 two Gaumont CHRONOs were installed. In 1916 the two Gaumonts were replaced with two motorised ERNEMANN II Projectors. The light sources were carbon arc likely of the same manufacturer. The increased length of films by 1916 required twin projector operation. Light sources for the Gaumont machines is not known and speculation of no value.

The 'sound' system remained for both original and extended cinemas was via phonograph and a piano.

The 1912 gas engine generator was 6.5hp giving out around 200watts of power.

The 1913 replacement was 12.7hp and capable of 1000watts of energy.

GLADYS EGAN, HENRY B. WALTHALL, JAMES
KIRKWOOD IN "A CONVICT'S SACRIFICE"

HERBERT YOST, LINDA ARVIDSON IN
"EDGAR ALLAN POE"

Scenes from typical films shown *circa* 1912. Each film would have been around 900 ft in length lasting barely 10minutes. *Authors collection*

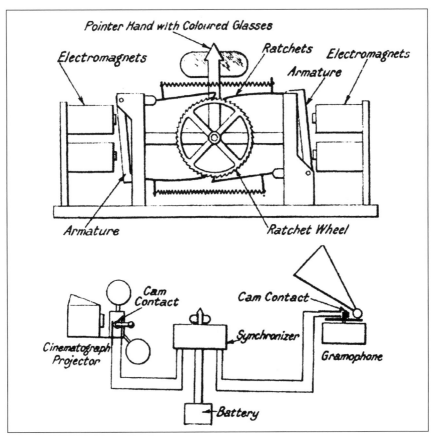

The Vivaphone Synchroniser. The Picture House ran 'sound synchronised' pictures as early as 1914 using a Vivaphone synchroniser developed by Cecil Hepworth. The results could be quite good though as with most of these systems the sound was recorded before the film was shot. *Courtesy of B.Brown*

PICTURE HOUSE, CLEVEDON.

Monday Next—"THE MENACING PAST" (2 Acts)
and "BRITAIN'S NEW ARMY IN TRAINING."

Thursday Next—"THIRTEEN DOWN" (2 Acts).
War Map showing Model Battle of Neuve Chapelle.

All the week, Charlie Chaplin Skill Competition
Nightly at 9.   Prizes from 5s. to £2 2s.
Come and see them, or better, try your skill at make-up.

Showing Nightly, 7—10.   MATINEES at 3 every Tuesday & Saturday.

This advertisement was for a week, the date not known. However, the interesting Item about the publicity is Charlie Chaplin Skill Competion Running all of the week at 9 pm with prizes nightly of 5/- to £2.2/-. Big prizes for the time. *Authors collection*

POST CARD

Kindly send this Card to your Friend.

Pathé Frères Cinema Ltd.; Series (Copyright)
PRINTED IN ENGLAND

THE EXPLOITS OF ELAINE
IS SHOWING AT THE
CLEVEDON PICTURE HOUSE
every Monday, Tuesday
:: and Wednesday. ::

*This is a Photograph of one of
the Chief Characters.*

You should just see this Serial. It
is proved to be the best ever produced.

Full of scientific and wonderfully
worked out situations, in which the
Hero and Heroine endure untold
vicissitudes.

CREIGHTON HALE

A picture postcard advertising a serial running at the Picture House in 1917. The leading man was Creighton Hale. *Courtesy of Barbara Connell*

ISSUED [APRIL 20th.

THE TOPICAL BUDGET
NEWS OF THE WORLD
IN ANIMATION

MARINE AEROPLANE
RACES AT MONACO.
FARMAN, VOISIN, CURTISS, FABRE,
and many others competing.

CUP FINAL TEAMS
Barnsley and West Bromwich Albion.

LOSS OF THE TITANIC
Memorial Service at St. Paul's Cathedral
Attended by Lord Mayor & Bishop of London.

Juvenile "Astronomers" Studying
ECLIPSE OF THE SUN
PRIMROSE DAY
Many visitors to Lord Beaconsfield's Statue.

Editorial Address: 50 GRAYS INN ROAD, LONDON, W.C.   34-2

MILES AHEAD IN EVERY RESPECT.

ISSUED APRIL 17th.

THE TOPICAL BUDGET
NEWS OF THE WORLD
IN ANIMATION

THE TITANIC
At SOUTHAMPTON, prior to her maiden
voyage, which has proved so disastrous.

SOUTH LONDON HARRIERS
hold a most successful meeting at the Oval.

The Entente Cordiale
FETE DAY AT CANNES
The Monument of the late King Edward
unveiled by the French Premier.

THE SHOPS ACT BILL
Protest Meeting in Trafalgar Square.

The White Star Line
Anxious crowds awaiting news outside the
London Office.

Editorial Address: 50 GRAYS INN ROAD, LONDON, W.C.   34-1

OUR LAST WEEK'S POSTERS.

Note the Release dates and compare them with others of the same date.

THE TOPICAL FILM CO.,
50, Gray's Inn Road, London, W.C.
Telephone: Holborn 5539.

'Topical Budget' newsreel publicity for 17/20 April 1920 *Authors collection*

4. The Second Picture House 1920 to 1922

By the coming of the 'Twenties' the little Picture House had outgrown itself. Cinema had become a part of life especially the working classes. Not only conversions of existing theatres and halls but brand new cinemas were being built up and down the country and apart from Bristol the nearest to Clevedon were at Weston-super-Mare, with the new Central Cinema (1921) in course of construction, and the Regent (1913) eventually to become the Gaumont. The infinite wonder of the 'living picture' had blossomed into the world of the movies and it was time for Victor Cox to exploit that for Clevedon.

To the east of the first Picture House was land owned by Albert Type who as mentioned earlier ran a horse and fly business at the rear end of the site known as Coly House Mews. The remainder was given over to trees and pasture. Albert Type lived in Coly House on the corner of Hillside Road and Old Church Road. He also ran a coal business with coal yards in Old Church Road and Coleridge Road North. By 1920 the horse and trap business was fast coming to an end as the motor car, and more dramatically the public transport omnibuses run locally by Richard Stevens, were providing mobility for the populace.

The remains of the Coly Mews can be easily distinguished today. Walking past what is the east end of the Curzon there is evidence of where the brickwork of the cinema ends and the stonework of the original Mews starts. Type would have kept most of his vehicles and horses here. There was a loose-box, harness room and eight stalls as well as the coach house. There was also a loft and the doors through which hay was lifted are still in place. The loft today is the home and studios of Curzon FM the local community radio station.

The mews and its surrounding pasture land became available and was acquired by the Clevedon Cinephone Company as the site for building of a new cinema. An announcement in the 'Mercury' for 6 March 1920 declared that:

the site next to the Picture House had been purchased and plans for alterations are of a very extensive character and it is safe to say that with the large addition to the ground space now in the possession of the Company Clevedon is to have a structure of which they will have every reason to be proud.

There was also a statement which said that during the construction of the new cinema it would not prevent the continuation of picture showing at the existing cinema.

The plans for the new cinema showed that it would have a balcony, café, dance floor, and lock-up shops. There would be facilities for stage shows and it would have boxes. The new cinema plans were imposing, grand and quite adventurous for a town with little more than 5,000 inhabitants.

Unbelievable as it seemed at the time, and does so today, picture showing continued throughout construction of the new cinema. Researching through the *Clevedon Mercury* from March 1920 to July 1922 not one week was missed, there being regularly two complete programmes throughout each week. This was further authenticated with the twice weekly serials in which there was no break in the continuity. This was probably done elsewhere in the country with a new cinema going up alongside the old. Indeed this was the case at Clevedon but in this instance the new cinema was being built horizontally over the old cinema.

Excavation and construction of the main shell of the new building began early in March 1920 continuing steadily as the new auditorium took shape. By July 1921 the first part of the construction and major fitting out had been completed and at this stage the operation was moved into the new cinema and picture showing in the first Picture House ceased. Interestingly the projection room of the new building could not have been built at that time because looking at it today it is situated over where the old cinema was and one can only assume that it was done with some temporary expediency employed. After the transfer work continued apace and by the end of September 1921 it was mostly finished.

The last film to show in the first Picture House is thought to be 'Anova, The Adventuress' (1919) starring Alma Taylor and the final episode of the serial 'Daredevil Jack'. The first in the new cinema was 'Smouldering Embers' (1919) with Frank Keenan and the start of a new serial 'The Adventures of Ruth'.

The cinema was indeed quite grand for the town of Clevedon, best described as Neo-classical, built with bricks from Sydney Keen's brickyard situated in Strode Road, his insignia embossed on each brick. Masonry, as well as the ornamental stone work, was provided from the J.N. Cox & Son masonry yard. The front, which is really the side, ran the length of the site along Old Church Road. One cannot say that it has great architectural merit but it is pleasing and is a building of its time. Today it has a Grade 2 listing.

The architecture would appear to be a design of mixed styles, however, for a town of Clevedon in the twenties it was to be quite a grand building. In the first week of March 1920 the once placid pasture where Albert Type's horses grazed became a building site. The tall trees were felled and the boarding went up behind which the construction of Clevedon's new Picture House started in earnest. There must have been much wonderment by residents of the town as bit by bit the structure

The splendid frontage of Picture House 2 completed in 1922. The picture portrays the cinema as it was built and allows interesting comparison with the changes throughout the years to the present day. *Courtesy of Clevedon Mercury*

took shape alongside the little cinema they had become so fond of and still visited as it continued its evening performances whilst the construction of its successor continued a-pace.

First to be seen were the tall pillars up to first floor level. There were eight of them including the two each end of the front elevation. These eight pillars of dressed stone formed the lower façade which was to include the shops and the entrances to the cinema. Above the first level rose eight more smooth pilasters topped with capitals in classic Ionic volutes. Above those a cornice parapet on which red brickwork ran the full length between the two pediment ends of the building which were also constructed in red brick. Finally the great expanse of the pitched roof of pantiles which covered the whole length and breadth of the building.

The remainder of the outer shell was in brick and the sheer size of the building alongside of the diminutive cinema it dwarfed must have raised a few eyebrows. The brick work on the west and east walls were pointed up in black mortar which

A recent picture shows some of the changes to the Picture House, now the Curzon, that have taken place over the years. The eastern entrance was where the first shop on the left of the picture is now. 'The Picture House' was engraved on each of the pediments. The western end was the same as the eastern end with a Lunette arched window destroyed in 1941.
Authors Collection

can still be seen today. Just what Albert Type must have thought as this edifice rose on his former land and virtually opposite Coly House can only be imagined.

The ground floor on the front elevation was to have two entrances one at the eastern end and the main one at the western end. Between the entrances there were five lock-up shops. The east entrance was further sub-divided to provide a sixth lock-up shop. Above on the first floor front between the 2nd and 7th pillars five tri-partite windows were placed each with decorative and smooth stone dressings Beneath the gabled ends Lunette (semi-circular) arched windows fit into a masonry arch from which the stonework fanned out around the arch resembling rays of the sun. All the windows contained stained glass thought to be orange and green. In the two pediments the words PICTURE HOUSE were engraved in stone and a flag-pole rose from the apex of each.. Later the name on the east pediment was changed to OAK ROOM CAFÉ and still exists today. The remaining lunette window looks to be of Critall construction which, to me, seems to be a little out of keeping with the wooden tri-partite windows.

The interior of the second Picture House in 1929. The newly installed organ can be seen in the box nearest the right-side of the proscenium. Note the absence of interior lighting fittings there just a string of lamps. There is no explanation available as to why this is so after nearly eight years of operation. *Late R. Pervis FRPS*

Internally the new cinema was quite a grand affair. By July 1921 the new auditorium was ready to open. I will describe the interior later but suffice it to say that enough of the new building was ready to be used and it is at this point that there is speculation as to how the move was done.

If one looks at the second cinema construction closely the new auditorium was quite simply on the pasture joining up with the Mews. The original cinema was at the West end and the new building abutted to it, but that was only the main auditorium. By the middle of 1921 the balcony had not yet been built as it was to be over the original cinema. Where was the projection room to the new cinema? As you can see today it is over the site of the old cinema. So how did the new cinema open before the old one closed?

The plans for the new building are sparse, if ever they existed, because it is legend that the whole building was drawn on the back of cigarette packets. No records can be found even reports of the opening are non-existent. A first guess seems to be that as the first cinema was quite low in height being between 24 ft and 30 ft and had a flat roof. The shell of the new one was built over it at around first floor level thus providing space for at least the projection room (in the position it is today). This is borne out by the fact that some interior decoration of the first cinema is still visible on the inside of the outer west wall. Hence the steps up to the auditorium.

As to the projection room. If you look at the thickness of the projection room floor this seems unlikely to have been achieved without closing off the original cinema. The best guess is that a temporary projection room was installed in the rear of the new auditorium until the proper existing one could be constructed. It will probably never be known quite how it actually was done. The 1921 projection room was considerably smaller than the present with a different layout for entrance and exit originating from the floor of the old cinema site.

There is clear evidence, however, that the new Picture House was built without any interruption to evening performances. It took twenty-seven months to build and records show proof the performances continued during that time. Therefore the cinema site can claim to be the oldest continuously operated one in the country.

In September 1921 the balcony was completed. It was 'free standing'. That is to say that it was supported at the rear and sides but had no supporting beams along the front. It opened without ceremony and by June 1922 the new cinema was complete with the Oak Room Café fitted out and open. Just who had actually built the new cinema is obscure. The only references being to Messrs Gardiner Ltd who supplied workers from their engineering firm in Bristol and Cardiff craftsmen who worked on the interior decoration. There were also workers from Taunton, Portishead and Swansea.

One entered the new cinema by two ways. The eastern entrance was for the cheaper stalls, probably known as the PIT and the larger western, and grander, entrance was for the rear stalls, the balcony and probably another entrance for theOak Room Café. The eastern entrance was of a simple layout and contained only a pay box and sweets stall. The western entrance foyer was a grand affair with the pay box in a central position, confectionery shop and couches. Steps took you up to the first floor landing, as now, and entrance to the rear stalls. More stairs then took one up to the Oak Room Café lounge area and upwards again to the balcony lounge, balcony, boxes and promenades.

A WONDERMENT

Entering the auditorium the delightful interior decoration met the eye. Like most other cinemas of the period the Picture House décor appeared to be of plaster-

Part of the barrel-vaulted ceiling. *Authors collection*

work, however, closer inspection revealed that it was in fact a series of embossed metal panels. An instant art work. It was put together on site and when painted had all the appearance of plaster-work. In those days it was probably a cheaper way of interior decoration of a hall or cinema because to engage sculpture plasterers was expensive. It is probable that other cinemas may have been decorated in this way. One has been discovered to have had this type of décor and that was the County Cinema at Warwick. When that cinema was demolished enough of the embossed plate was salvaged and now adorns the barrel-vaulted ceiling in Ashorn Organ Museum in near Warwick. Another cinema, the Radway in Sidmouth, has a similar metal panelled ceiling.

It is possible that the embossed metal plate may have come from America as there is evidence that a similar form of interior décor was quite widespread there. It is also known that a similar product was produced in South Wales. As craftsmen from Cardiff were working on the project it is possible that the embossed plate décor came from SouthWales, however as Cardiff was a busy port and ships using it came from America it is also possible that it was an import from the USA.

Rear of the cinema showing the original Albert Type mews. This area is likely for redevelopment of cinema facilities. *Authors collection*

Another view of the eastern end of the cinema. The 'join' of the old Picture House' to the part that was originally the Mews with the hay loft doors can clearly be seen. *Authors collection*

One of the shop units in 1923. Standing
in the doorway is the proprietor Mr. J.
Blackmore. *Courtesy R. Blackmore*

The Oak Room lounge in 1923. Pictured is the
stained glass window, destroyed by enemy action
in 1941. The floor covering seems to have been
linoleum with a carpet. The lady and little girl are
unknown. *Photo Victor Cox courtesy of Jane Lilly*

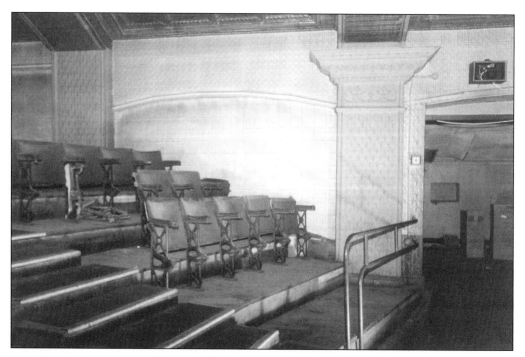

This picture shows some of the remaining seating in the long closed Balcony. The decorative
metal panelling is clearly shown. The Original entry to the Balcony was by the stepped aisle
and the Exit-way led to the Balcony toilets. *Authors collection*

The 'Music Box' Chicago, USA. The façade of this cinema dates back to the early 1920's and the front is metal panelling thought to be similar to that of the Picture House interior-hence the possible American connection. The 'Music Box' is still operating today.
Coutesy of C. Preece

PICTURE HOUSE
OLD CHURCH ROAD CLEVEDON PHONE 58

Monday Tuesday Wednesday May 31st. June 1st & 2nd.

Mrs. Charles Chaplin

BORROWED CLOTHES

ALSO OUR POPULAR SERIAL - EPISODE 9

THE RED GLOVE

*

Thursday Friday Saturday   June 3rd. 4th. 5th.

A Special Realist Melodrama

WANTED - A MOTHER

Episode 4 of the exciting serial

THE LIGHTENING RAIDER

and the Cartoon TRAMP TRAMP TRAMP

Daily from 5.30pm-10pm. No Matinees due to building

A handbill advertising films for the week 31 May 1920. Note how Mildred Harris (Chaplins first wife) is billed. *Authors collection*

The Welsh firm from which it is thought the embossed metal panelling could have come from was the Grovesend Tinplate Works at Gorseinon who are known to have manufactured a panelling similar to that found in the Clevedon cinema. It is believed that the Grovesend company was diverse in the products it manufactured and this type of metal décor was not, likely, a leading product. So the origin of the unique décor covering the interior of the auditorium remains a matter of conjecture. Here, it has to be recorded, the efforts of Keith Morgan, Curator of the Trostre Works Cottage and Industrial Museum at Llanelli for his work to establish the origin of material.

The embossed metal plate came in a series of patterns and sizes some being quite plain, others with embossed edges and centres and others quite large with more intricate patterns and reliefs. Battens were fixed to the virgin brick wall interiors and the specially prepared supports for the ceiling. With the notion similar to a giant jigsaw, the ceiling and walls were constructed by nailing the individual embossed panelling to them from a pre-conceived pattern. On completion it was decorated in a multitude of colours ranging from reds, blues and greens to orange and gold. The base colour was predominantly cream with reliefs in the panelling picked out on Gold. Dado panels and the skirting were in light and dark grey. The ceiling was probably the same as the walls with the relief-work in Gold. The proscenium arch, its pediment and much of the relief work in the panelling was done out also in gold. The doors were Brown and had Japanese glass panels.

It is preserved, more or less, in its entirety and today is considered the best example of this type of art-deco form of interior décor not only in the UK but probably in the world.

One cannot imagine that it was really a cheap form of décor for it must have taken many hours to complete and was labour intensive. However, as no other known complete example of such cinema interior décor design has been discovered it is quite rare although it is understood that there is a cinema in Illinois, USA existing today which has a similar design of embossed metal plate adorning the exterior fascia.

COMPLETION

When the balcony was completed the cinema had 804 seats arranged over stalls and balcony the best being of maroon plush, the cheaper front stalls being of hard forms. The proscenium was 32 ft wide and the stage had a depth of around 17ft Full stage facilities provided a trap door, two dressing rooms and an orchestra pit. There was a fly gallery though no fly tower. Full stage lighting was installed with floats, footlights and lights each side of the stage installed behind the proscenium arch. The screen was fitted to a frame on the back wall of the stage. The frame exists today.

The stalls were, and are, deeply raked necessary of course when one considers it was built to rise above the old cinema. The balcony was similarly seated with an entrance from the rear and exit, with access to the boxes to the right. An exit to the left led to the promenade, boxes and toilets. The front of the circle was a posh affair with the best seats in the house, bar the loge seats, and it was really a Grand Circle. The loge seats were for the lesser VIPs, such as traders of the town, and situated within an alcove at the rear of the balcony. One of these seats was equipped with a hearing aid, the only one in the house although surely another system must have been installed later. The loge seats were probably one of the least comfortable positions in the whole auditorium for viewing the screen.

The barrel-vaulted ceiling was without doubt the main feature of the interior. Moulded in the metal plate patterns it is quite a work of art. Along with the theatrical proscenium arch it must have given the feeling of elegance to the patrons of the day. Various alterations have not disturbed the décor too much and it is well worth a visit to the cinema just to see it even though the balcony is not in use now.

To each side of the upper auditorium there were three balcony level boxes each with an ornate semi-circular balustrade. Behind the boxes were promenades each made private with gold and maroon curtains with swags of material at the front. The boxes could seat three to five persons but were only used on special occasions or for concerts. They had no permanent seats and when in use chairs were brought from the Old Oak Café. It is said that patrons could sit in the boxes when films were showing.

There are some amusing tales about the building of the new Picture House. Mr Harry Edwards relates how, whilst working for Gilbert Hendy, a Clevedon builder, he volunteered to paint the proscenium arch with gold paint, real gold at about £20 a gallon in those days. He did the 'piece across the top' standing on the top of a ladder. Health and Safety at Work was unheard of then. The firm also painted the whole of the panelling and any loose panels were held back by nails driven into the battens behind. Another amusing occurrence was when a seedling tree sprang up through the tiled floor in one exit way on the ground floor. It is said that it was left for years to grow?

With the new cinema well and truly opened without any special ceremony the work continued on the Oak Room Café and the final fitting out. By June 1922 this was open and the project to build this new cinema was complete. (The Oak Room Café is dealt with in Chapter 11.) It is reported in the Kinematograph Year books of those early years that there was a dance hall. There was mention of this in the sparse details available of the original 'plans' but no record that one was actually built. The compilation of the Year books relied mostly upon cinema owners reporting the details of their premises for publication and in many cases these were not up dated. Likely there were dancing facilities provided for in the Café in the early days. Who knows?

The lock-up shops were by this time occupied. The first to take a shop was George Eddy who opened a boot and shoe store in No. 1. Later in life George Eddy became the steward of the Liberal Club in the Triangle and was, it is reported, very popular locally. For a time Strode Road Garage had a retail outlet in No. 2. Other occupants of the shop units included a music and piano shop run by Mr Dark, known as Daddy Dark to the boys who attended Sunday School at St. John's, who apparently used to bang with great might on the piano when accompanying the hymns.

There was a turf accountants run by Mr Poncione who was described as a loudly dressed bookie and the remaining two lock-ups were an antiques shop and a sweets shop.

At the beginning of 1923 the music shop was replaced by an electrical and wireless store run by the Blackmore family. There is a photograph in existence showing that J.N. Cox had one of the units for a time as a reception area for his monumental masonry business.

5. 1923 to 1930

The second Picture House was at once extremely popular. The sceptics were proved wrong and patrons thronged to the new cinema. Virtually all vestiges of the first cinema were gone by now and those that remained were in the 'vaults' of the new building and remain so to this day.

This period was perhaps the most interesting of the cinema's life. Some of the films that were shown and the coming War years are dealt with in later chapters but throughout the next two decades important changes to the cinema centred mainly upon the coming of the talkies and the eventual sale.

For the first eleven years the rebuilt Picture house was on silent film. For 3d. (if you sat on the hard seats at the front of the stalls) 6d. 9d. or 1/- in the stalls, 1/6d. or 2/- (pre-booked) in the balcony you were entertained by a programme of shorts and a feature film often with the stars of the day Charles Chaplin, Rudolph Valentino, Harry Langdon, Nazimova, Douglas Fairbanks and so many others. The audiences cheered, clapped the heroes and hissed at the villains, as was then the custom and when a particular popular film was being shown like Chaplins 'Gold Rush' the house was packed to capacity.

Sound was many years away. Accompaniment to the silent films was usually provided by the piano situated in the orchestra pit. The phonograph, replaced by a gramophone, still sitting on the instrument and used to play during the intervals and to give the musician(s) a rest. It had a large horn necessary to drive the sound into the auditorium. It was also used to provide background music to the Gaumont Graphic newsreels and other shorts.

The piano was played for many years by Mrs Pegram, who lived in Kenn Road, Gelly Somerton and often by Victor Cox himself. For the more prestigious of films a small Bijou orchestra would be formed and for really important films a fourteen piece orchestra filled the small orchestra pit. Vocalists were also called in to perform arias and duets either as support to the scenes being enacted on the screen or during interludes. Often Victors stepmother, stage name Blanche Harwood, would render classical and popular songs to the images on the screen.

Sound effects were also provided on stage in the wings which was a favourite trick of cinemas in the silent days. Drums, whistles, shouts and even chains being dragged about were all part of the show. On one occasion it is recorded that the sound of an organ was required for a dramatic religious episode so the harmonium from St John's School across the way was dragged across the road to the cinema. It was no match for the instrument portrayed in the film but was played with great gusto and gave a good account of itself.

In 1929 Victor Cox commissioned an organ for the Picture House, no doubt to counter the new cinemas in Bristol. It is thought to have been installed by Daniel and Son, organ builders of Clevedon. It was situated in the right hand box nearest to the stage. This location could not have been ideal for accompaniment to films. It was most probably used for concerts, recitals and interval music etc. With the orchestra pit still in use this was probably the next best position. The organ was played by Mrs Morris, who was organist at St John's Church. This lady was a most versatile musician and was best known as Enid Payne, her maiden name, for her piano recitals on radio. Victor Cox played the instrument from time to time for many years. The organ remained in the cinema for fourteen years and was removed in 1943. It found a home in a village chapel at Winscombe. There is also mention that there was a second organ installed, this time at the front of the stage. There is no actual record of this though the date is said to be 1933–34 and unfortunately nothing has been found identifying this second organ. Hopes are high that history will repeat itself as consideration is being given towards installing a heritage cinema organ in the future plans.

Today it is difficult to capture in the mind what going to the cinema was like in the early twenties before the 'talkie' era. Those years and right back to the near beginnings we speak of the 'silent' years. Well perhaps the film was mute but little else was. To illustrate the point I would like to repeat a passage from a previous book in which I describe 'silent cinema'.

Cinemas were *never* silent. What the films lacked in audibility the cinema environment made up for. The thuds as the tip-up seats went down as they were sat upon or sprang back as they were freed (there were no rubber 'silencers' in those days). The click of the piano reading light as it was switched on. In the projection room the clatter of the primitive projectors as they drove the film relentlessly forward could often be heard in the auditorium. The rattle of the piano player's rings and bangles as she raised the tempo to the action on the screen. The hiss of the hygienic spray as it was carried around the auditorium spelling death to any germs – and the patrons dandruff. The rustle of sweets being extracted from paper bags, and the sucking of lollipops. The occasional snore, more if the film was boring and at the end the renewed clatter and bang of the tip-up seats when THE END was expected to appear on the screen, only to recede momentarily when it did not and most of all the hisses and boos of the audience matched only by the 'sound effects' coming from backstage.

Add to this the reaction to the occasional film break or technical hitch that confronted the skill of the projectionist as he would struggle to get the picture back on the screen, is almost legendary. Silent cinema? That it certainly never was!

One other point that only came to mind recently when the carpet was replaced in the Curzon. Beneath the old carpet was linoleum still well preserved and unlike the paper-thin material of today was heavy and solidly backed. Carpeting was, in 'silent' days, a real luxury found in the most lavishly furnished cinemas. No so in the Picture House if our find is authentic so imagine the plod of feet up and down the aisles during the performances on a hard linoleum surface. Contrary to belief the advent of the 'talkies' actually quietened the cinemas and the Picture House would have been no exception.

The new cinema gained even more popularity and soon the thoughts of it as being too grand for a town of a mere 5,000 souls was quickly dispelled for it also attracted folk from miles around. Life at the cinema was a rarely dull and it was run to a high standard by Victor Cox. Often Victor would be found in the Pit entrance pay box whilst his stepmother would be in the plush seats entrance at the other end of the building. She still occasionally sang, especially if the films were patriotic or religious in content, and Victor played the piano when called upon.

Famous celebrities visited from time to time and they included Henry B. Irvine (Sir Henry's son) an actor who appeared in a few silent films and Betty Balfour, a popular comedy actress of silent days. There were concerts from time to time. The first advertised one was for Sunday, 13 January 1929 when the inauguration of the organ took place and was played by Mrs Morris. A second concert followed on 10 March.

Around this time pantomimes were staged. The first was on 7 February. 1929 when 'Sinbad The Sailor' was staged with full orchestra and chorus. Others followed. In late December of the same year 'Mother Goose' was staged and the following year 'The Forty Thieves'. Sunday concerts became a regular feature. On 29 September 1929 Gertrude Ford, a well-known singer, appeared on the stage supported by Mr E. Richard's dog act and there was a special Sunday concert held on 16 February 1930 when Jordan L. Duis brought his Symphony Orchestra to the Picture House. Cine-Variety made its debut in July of that year with a concert called 'Frivolity Revels' plus a film.

The film fare remained very much the same as before with the emphasis on British films. Hollywood 'blockbusters' did find their way on to the screen, albeit a few years after release, and stars like Rudolf Valentino, Buster Keaton, Charles

Chaplin, to name a few, filled the house at every performance when their films were shown. In those days a performance was continuous from 5.30 nightly and finished about 10.30 pm There were matinees on Tuesday and Saturday at 2.30 pm

By 1927 sound had arrived and the cinema industry revolutionised by the new wonder. The Picture House was soon experimenting with the new fledgling.

2ND GRAND
Sunday Concert

AT THE

PICTURE HOUSE, CLEVEDON,

— on —

SUNDAY, MARCH 10, at 8.15 p.m.

Prices as usual.   Children in arms not admitted.
Children under 12 admitted with adults only.

PROGRAMME.

1. Organ Solo   " SELECTED "
   Mrs. MORRIS, L.R.A.M., Leipzig

2. Song   " TOREADOR SONG " from " Carmen "
   Mr. ROBERT ROWLANDS, Baritone

3. Violin Solo   " RODINO "   Beethoven, arr. Kreisler
   Mr. E. J. TREVELYN

4. Song   " I HEARD YOU SINGING "   Eric Coates
   Miss M. COCKSEDGE, Contralto

5. Monologue   Bransby Williams
   " THE GREEN EYE OF THE YELLOW GOD "
   Miss H. S. KELLY

6. Harp Solo   " SELECTED "
   Miss DOROTHY GODWIN, A.R.A.M.

7. Song   " FISHERMEN OF ENGLAND "
   from " The Rebel Maid "
   Mr. ROBERT ROWLANDS, Baritone

8. Violin Solo   " CELEBRATED SERENATA "   E. Toselli
   Mr. E. J. TREVELYN

9. Song   " LITTLE BROWN BIRD SINGING "
   Hadyn Wood
   Miss M. COCKSEDGE, Contralto

10. Monolgue   " DEVIL MAY CARE "   Bransby Williams
    Miss H. S. KELLY

11. Harp Solo   " SELECTED "
    Miss DOROTHY GODWIN, A.R.A.M.

Subject to alteration at the discretion of the Management.

G. E. Hancock, Limited, Clevedon.

Programme for the second Sunday Concert following the inauguration of the organ.
Courtesy G.E. Hancock

6. The 'Talkies'

The 'talkies' found their way into cinemas after years of experimentation. There were many variations of systems to add sound to films in the early years. Sound linked to picture was first used in the Picture House as early as 1914 when. 'Pictures with sound' were advertised for the week of 6 April of that year. 'Hard Cash' a drama in two parts and 'The Outlaw' a western also in two parts were shown as 'pictures with sound' for the first half of the week. The second half was billed as 'Musgrave Ritual', a Sherlock Holmes picture, and another thriller 'The Silver Skull' both in two parts and were they were also presented as 'pictures with sound'.

The Picture House however was rather late in going over to 'talkies'. Legend has it that in 1927 Victor Cox engaged 'a man from the North' to install a Vitaphone sound system into the cinema. Other than a couple of references in past writings about the cinema I can find no factual records to support the date but if there was such a sound system installed it certainly was not Vitaphone.

Experiments to link sound to 'living pictures' had been around as long as cinematography itself. As early as 1889 Edison, and William Dickson, had achieved a rough synchronisation of sound to picture for his Kinetograph. William Friese-Greene, and many others had designed devices for coupling sound to image before 1900. Around that time Leon Gaumont had produced the Chronophone and one minute 'sound shorts' of great stars of the theatre, opera and ballet were being produced. In Britain the Chronophone proved very popular as did Englishman Cecil Hepworth's Vivaphone. Oskay Messtar of Germany was supplying recorded musical scores for his films by 1908.

All of these systems used wax disks, mechanically recorded, and the gramophone sound 'amplified' by a large horn. There were major problems however which were not finally solved until towards the end of the 1920s when synchronisation of sound to picture, amplification and the development of electronic valve had been developed.

By the mid 1920s there was much activity again to produce sound to picture. By this time radio had taken the high ground in entertainment and the silent picture was under threat. Experiments with disks and electric recording was pioneered by Berliner and by 1925 Western Electric and Bell Telephone laboratories in America had produced a sound on disk system which they called Vitaphone. It was at first shunned by the major studios but in 1926 the then lesser studio Warner Brothers formed the Vitaphone Corporation with the intention of

The sound stage of Warner Bros. Vitaphone production of "The Singing Fool" (1928) starring Al Jolson (extreme right). The camera is imprisoned in its sound-proof booth.
Authors collection

A vintage amplifier installed in cinemas in the early years of sound.
Authors collection

Publicity blurb for Warner Bros. Vitaphone talking pictures 1928 produced to combat imitations.
Authors collection

Early talkies. An early phonograph used in biographs and early cinemas it was wildly synchronised to the projector to provide music and effects. *Authors collection*

Early projector fitted with Vitaphone sound-on-disk and Photophone optical sound equipment. This projector is on display in the Curzon's collection of heritage projectors.
Authors collection

A 'talkie' installed projection room 1929. Note the disk unit at the rear of the projector. *Authors collection*

providing synchronised musical accompaniment to all of their films making it possible for cinemas which had no full orchestra to have just that to accompany Warner's films.

Vitaphone was a 16 inch platter record, one record to each reel of silent film, played by a device attached and synchronised to the film projector and using a thermonic valve amplifier to reproduce the sound 'track' from a speaker behind the screen.

A projector with such a device can be seen in the collection of heritage projectors displayed in the Curzon.

The first such production to have Vitaphone was 'Don Juan' (1926) and it was premiered at Warner Theatre in 52nd Street, New York on 6 August 1926. The next film scheduled to have Vitaphone was of course 'The Jazz Singer' (1927) with Al Jolson risking all in what has become to be known as the first talking picture. It was however only part talkie with little more than 250 words of spoken dialogue in addition to the musical numbers and then the film lapsed back into silence. The first talkie using Vitaphone advertised as a 100% talking picture was 'Lights Of New York' (1928).

Not wanting this to be a history lesson about sound systems I will only briefly mention that by 1928 a system whereby sound was 'photographed' and placed alongside the image on the film had arrived (Movietone and Photophone and developed by William Fox and by RCA using experiments and patents already existing) which placed the sound in solid synchronisation with picture and was known as optical sound. Within a few years or so it had completely replaced Vitaphone on talkie pictures. It is the method used to this day.

So what of the Picture House and the story of Vitaphone being installed in 1927 by the 'man from the North'?

I have already mentioned the 'pictures with sound' that were shown in 1914 and probably there were others. These would almost certainly have been shown using a Hepworth's VIVAPHONE which was in fact very good though there were some problems for an inexperienced operator. The apparatus was linked to the projector by a synchroniser which in turn controlled the gramophone by the screen. Used mainly for accompanied music and narration it worked well and it seems that such films were welcomed by patrons to the Picture House.

It is said that in 1927, certainly before the introduction of Warner Brothers Vitaphone to Britain, Victor Cox and a 'man from the North' had installed sound apparatus in the Picture House.

It could not have been a Vitaphone system. Vitaphone was owned by Warner Brothers and could not be used by anyone else world-wide. It was a term obviously used to describe any sound-by-disk system of which happened to be around at the time.

Victor Cox would have been hard pressed to install Vitaphone in 1927. It would have cost him upwards of £20,000, even if were freely available in this country to a small concern such as the Picture House in its first year of introduction. To finally prove the point Victor Cox would have had to play Warner Bros pictures at the cinema more or less exclusively and no other product. Records show he did not.

Considering the cost of installing the real Vitaphone system and the conditions that applied the erudite Victor Cox probably turned to the legendary 'man from the North' and I suggest that this was later than 1927. Research has turned up two possibilities.

The Imperial Sound System originated from both Leicester and Loughborough. The Electrokhord system of Leeds and Halifax and possibly a third called Picturetone were active in 1928 or so. The 'expert from the North' may have been one of these involved in producing a sound system for the Picture House and this is quite possible. Either way there is unfortunately no confirmation that 'talkies' were being shown at the Picture House at that time and those that may have been were either musical shorts or comedy shorts produced in Britain. These would probably have included one-reelers such as 'Cavaleria Rusticana', or 'The Raw Recruit' starring musical hall star Ernest Latinga and short comedies by George Robey and other artistes of the day who are known to have made one-reel 'talkies' on disk. The Picture House did not show a full length talkie until 1930 by which time it had been wired for both sound-on-disk and sound-on-film. Victor Cox is attributed to be the first to show talkies in the area but they would have been confined to home-spun shorts. To buy Hollywood was probably an option Victor would not have contemplated with a .non-Vitaphone system.

In 1930 the cinema was re-equipped with new projection equipment and wired for sound. Two Zeis projectors were installed with both sound-on-disc and sound-on-film apparatus (see Technical information at the end of this chapter).

The first full length feature film to be shown was 'The Grand Parade' (1930) and opened on 20 October 1930. It starred Helen Twelvetrees and was produced by Pathe Exchange. It was a sound-on-film (Photophone) picture and described as being a romantic drama containing minstrel shows, burlesque, alcoholism, marriage, pregnancy, religion and featured the city of Detriot. They certainly knew how to pack a story in those days although there is little notice of its existence.

Helen Twelvetrees was not well known in this country though she was listed as a leading lady in Hollywood. She was one of the first 'talkie' stars her first film being 'The Ghost Talks' (1929) and she remained in pictures until the end of the thirties. Interestingly 'The Grand Parade' does not appear in the lists. It was, however, an instant success at the Picture House with queues and extra shows all of that week. The following week the Clevedon cinema was back on silent film.

The cinema had always been 'late' with films 'The Grand Parade' being an exception to the rule. It was only when, by 1931/2, silent film production had completely ceased and as far as the Picture House was concerned, the backlog used up, did the complete changeover to talkies become apparent. There is no record of any of the well-known sound pictures having been played, too costly, and the first one of any note was in 1933 when Al Jolson's 'The Singing Fool' (1928) played to packed houses it being much cheaper to rent then I suppose. Booking systems were different in those days but Victor Cox nearly always played British films as opposed to Hollywood, likely because they were cheaper and because he seemingly used the booking services of Oswald Stoll who built the Bristol Hippodrome in St Augustine's Parade and had also acquired the Bedminster Hippodrome in East Street when it was a Music Hall in 1915 and converted it into a fine cinema complete with an orchestral organ.

The Stoll, Bedminster was destroyed by enemy action in 1941. It was a second run house so any Hollywood films were at least a couple of years or more behind the original release by the time they were shown there but for the British product that cinema benefited from its London owner by having a steady flow of recent pictures. The Bristol Hippodrome was also on films from 1932 until 1938.

Clevedon Picture House bookings were likely to have followed those of the Bedminster house although with no specific proof this may be conjecture. More recent research has suggested that film booking for the Picture House was connected with Moss Empires who had an office in Bristol, possibly at the old Bristol Empire Theatre. The Empire in Old Market was also on films between 1931 and 1939.

7. 1930 to 1945

Through the 1930s and 40s Victor Cox ran the Picture House to a high standard. Victor Cox was, however, a hard task-master. George Diamond worked in the Picture House in the early thirties. Both he and Mr Bart Price were 'button boys', so called for the rows of buttons running down the front of their tunics. They wore small pill-box hats with a chin strap. (this is disputed however). The Button Boys worked as ushers and one of the positions for the Boys was by the East entrance. On a signal from the projection room the Boy on duty would crawl through a trap door to the stage wings and then open up the front tabs (curtains) by ropes. When the show had started one Button Boy would report to the projection room to take up duties as rewind boy, tea maker and other odd jobs that started a career in a projection room whilst the remaining Boy would busy himself around the cinema under the watchful eye of Victor Cox.

In the early thirties there were five Button Boys employed. In addition to George and Bart Price there was Fred Hill, Roy Price and Alfie Hill, Fred Price was 'top boy' and received 2/6d. per week. The others received 2/-. For this they worked from 5.30 pm until 11 pm George remembers the projectionists at the time being Stan Newton and Douglas Price. It seems to be very much a family tradition to work at the Picture House in those days.

There was a 'hearing aid' system in one loge seat at the rear of the balcony and it was a Button Boys job to connect this up to the system. George remembers a Mr Cousins, who was a dentist in the town, paying him 3d. every time he visited the cinema on account of George 'wiring for sound'.

On the days films were delivered from London they arrived at around 4 am. They had to be wound on to the spools by hand by the Button Boys later that day and run through by the projectionists.

George also remembers that there were pantomimes in 1933 and 1934 those being Mother Goose and Ben Hur respectively. I respect George's recollections but a pantomime about Ben Hur seems somewhat bizarre. Both shows were staged by a professional company from London. It is from George that the recollection of a second organ being at the foot of the stage is gained. He also remembers that the music played for the intervals was on 78 rpm records and four were supplied by Seeley's Music Shop each week for which suitable recognition by way of a slide advertisement was shown on the screen.

Seat prices at this time were Stalls: 4d. on the hard seats at the front, 6d. for the first 4 rows of upholstered seats, 9d. for the next four rows and 1/2d for the rear stalls seats. The Balcony was 1s. 6d.

Publicity for the cinema programmes was through the local 'Mercury', by hand bills and posters. Programmes were also publicised somewhat uniquely by Reg Youde who paraded a sandwich board on wheels around the town. Around this time also the Commissionaire was Jack Sims who was also a taxi man and no doubt found further employment at the end of the show.

The stage was gained from the dressing rooms by a gallery and trap door on the actors left side of the stage. Quite how they managed dressed up in a variety of stage costumes, is anybody's guess but looking at the stage today one wonders how a full company was staged anyway.

The Picture House stayed much the same until 1939. Weekly programmes were split Monday to Wednesday and Thursday to Saturday. Films could not be shown on Sundays in those days unless they were of a serious religious nature. Concerts continued spasmodically. I have never been able to understand quite why it was acceptable to have a concert, which was indeed entertainment, on Sundays and yet the showing of films was considered unacceptable. Cinema-going was a 'habit' in those days and it provided cheap entertainment for the masses, especially the working class, and the Picture House was no exception. As the shows were continuous from 5.30 pm and 2.30 pm on Saturdays the feature film would be played twice and the supporting feature and programme once (Saturdays three times and twice) so if you were not in the cinema by 7.30 in the evening you would miss some of the programme or if you were in at 5.30 pm you could see the main feature twice if that was your quest but beware if you were noticed by a sharp eyed member of staff.

The years of War are dealt with in the following chapter but the cinema continued in much the same way until 1945 when Victor Cox, by then 58 years of age, sold the cinema and spent the remainder of his time with the family Monumental Masonry business. He also spent much of his time doing good works about the town.

Apparently Victor Cox did not have it all his own way as there was a rival bid to build another cinema in the town on a site in Woodlands Road in 1937. The plans were apparently approved until Cox, and a businessman, with whom he had connections and who was also a prominent Councillor, scuppered them. By what method this was achieved is not recorded.

In 1937 also plans were submitted for a complete redecoration of the interior. The result were some colour changes to the original with mauve above the boxes,

The projection room of the second Picture House *circa* 1930 when 'talkie' equipment was installed in the cinema. The sound-on-disk unit is seen lower left. *Authors collection*

THE OAK ROOM CAFE

MAIN ENTRANCE
PICTURE HOUSE.

OPEN FROM 10-30 a.m.
to 8-0 p.m.

LUNCHEONS
TEAS ... ...
SUPPERS ...

MODERATE CHARGES.

THE

Picture House

OLD CHURCH ROAD
CLEVEDON.
Phone—Clevedon 58.

AT 6-30 NIGHTLY.

Matinees Wednesday and
Saturday at 2-30 p.m.
Full Programme.

ATTRACTIONS for AUGUST, 1934.

TALKIES IN IDEAL
SURROUNDINGS

SEATS 7d. to 1/6 including tax.

POINTS WORTH KNOWING

Chocolates, Cigarettes, Ices and Teas are sold in the Theatre during the performance. Any attendant will instruct the Waitress to take your orders.

Doctors, Nurses, Business Gentlemen, etc. expecting Telephone Calls are invited to leave their names at the Pay-Box on entering when they will be called if desired.

Ventilation. Particular care is exercised daily as to the ventilation of the Theatre during the Summer months.

Oak Room Cafe open to the public daily (Sundays excepted) from 10-30 to 8 p.m.

Picture House

OLD CHURCH ROAD
CLEVEDON.
Phone—Clevedon 58.

AT 6-30 NIGHTLY.

Matinees Wednesday and
Saturday at 2-30 p.m.
Full Programme.

ATTRACTIONS FOR NOVEMBER, 1936.

TALKIES IN IDEAL
SURROUNDINGS

SEATS 6d. to 1/6 including tax.

Two examples of monthly programme cards given to patrons.

buttresses done out in off-white, balcony rails and box balustrades in red. Dado panelling, architraves and skirting received a dark blue and more notably the barrel-vaulted ceiling was done in bronze as it appears today. Doors remained brown.

Technical

From the opening in 1921/2 ERNEMAN II projectors were installed. They are reported to have been *in situ* in 1927 and later when short 'talkies' were shown on occasion.

The sound-on-disk system at that time was either an Electrochord or Imperial.

During the WW2 years two Ernemann projectors were in use so it is said however in 1930, according to the photograph, two ZEIS IKON projectors fitted with Zeis arc lamps, Vitaphone sound-on-disk unit and Photophone sound-on-film optical sound heads were *in situ*. The sound system was PICTURETONE.

In the 1940s the sound system was BRITISH TALKING PICTURES and this seems to have remained until 1945 at least.

GB speakers were installed at the rear of the stage in a Roxy Box.. The screen was on a wooden frame fixed to the back wall.

Clevedon's population in 1937 was 7,035.

It is known, however, that the two lamps were converted to PEERLESS MAGNARCS by 1944. The sound system was still British Talking Pictures (by now British Accoustic). There is also reference to a Picturetone sound system which was replaced in 1937 to British Talking Pictures (BTP) and remained as such until the introduction of Cinemascope in 1956.

Unfortunately there are so many conflicting reports of what projection equipment did actually inhabit the projection room that it is difficult to mention them all.

8. Years of War

In the summer of 1914 world events had turned the charming and elegant pastimes that could be enjoyed, by some that is, in Clevedon to one of fervent activity and patriotic feeling. Many of its young men were off to the biggest adventure of their lives, or so they thought. That summer, as had been the practice for years, saw the little town swell with bustling visitors to its beach and pier.

A little over two years after the little Picture House had first opened it was showing on its screen the events in Europe that were to lead to some of the most horrific pictures yet shown to audiences in Clevedon. Through the regular reports portrayed in the Gaumont Graphic and Topical Budget newsreels produced in the early months audiences could identify with the mood afoot in the Country and believing that the conflict would soon be over and our forces would be home victorious in a short while. All too soon the newsreels were showing the carnage and humiliation of the Great World War. This of course was the first time many people were to see moving pictures of War on their doorstep as it were and which involved people they knew had gone with others to fight. As time passed the weekly portrayal on the screen conditioned the audiences somewhat to what they would see each time they went to the cinema. Throughout the years of the War this was alleviated in some way by seeing the early screen 'stars' such as Lilian Gish, Roscoe 'Fatty' Arbuckle or some of Chaplin's first shorts.

More likely though because of Cox's policy of showing British films on the bill in preference to the product from Hollywood the likes of Alma Taylor, a popular actress with the Clevedon audiences, Betty Balfour and Stewart Rome to name a few would be the regular diet. Pictures such as 'A Munitions Girls Romance' and 'A Boy Scouts Life' all patriotic films, were very popular. Clevedon had assumed the mantle of a 'garrison town' with regiments such as the East Lancashires billeted at Kingston Seymour and the cinema was very busy indeed.

In 1939 it was somewhat different because War was expected and on that Sunday morning in September the mood was more sombre with those who were at the beach or on the pier perhaps reflecting that defences would shortly replace their presence and that things would not be the same again.

The Picture House, along with all cinemas, theatres and sports venues in the country closed down by Government decree on Sunday, 3 September the day War was declared with Nazi Germany. Growing fears that Hitler might bomb our cities the way he had Warsaw during the first days of War prompted the

Government to take this step to prevent a great loss of life with venues being targets of bombing raids should similar attacks against Britain take place. This did not materialise and in fact there began a period which became known as the 'phoney war'. Realising that entertainment, particularly cinema and sport, would maintain public morale the order was lifted at the end of the first week of the war and entertainment venues informed that they could re-open as from Monday, 11 September. The times of opening, however, were restricted to performances ending by 10pm, and starting earlier in the day, a requirement which was to last until shortly before the end of the war.

Most cinemas were able to re-open with little trouble whereas the theatres were hit quite hard with the loss of performers and the break up of shows due to the call up. Just about every cinema in the country played patriotic films during that first week. The film vaults were emptied of films about British derring-do, historic sagas in fact anything that would stir the hearts and minds of the picture-goers. The Picture House was no exception and was showing 'Q Planes' (1939) which starred Ralph Richardson, Laurence Olivier and Valerie Hobson. A British picture which told the story of spies stealing aircraft by a secret ray. It was a lively comedy-thriller and C.J. Lejune, a film critic of the time, described it as *a bright vigorous little picture, Mr Richardson's Major is the brightest thing in it. You should see it. You will like it. It has savour.*

Well the picture-goers of Clevedon took him at his word and flocked to the cinema filling the 800 seats every night of the week it ran. It must have been quite a scoop for Victor Cox for it was only months after its release and not years as was usually the case. Though it has to be said the film was probably booked for that date anyway. The performance times were in accordance with regulations and more use was made of the earlier part of the day.

Like other public places the Picture House prepared for war. Blackout precautions were put into place across the entrances. Glass was protected from splintering with the application of tape, Exterior signage was shut down for the duration and all illuminated publicity removed. It was difficult sometimes to tell whether the cinema was open or closed after dark but of course the patrons knew. To save paper the publicity posters were cut in size and more reliance placed upon the press for publicity.

It would appear that only a few of the personnel of the Picture House were affected by the call up but those still there no doubt formed themselves into fire-watchers to protect the cinema should any conflagration take place whilst others were doing their bit in the Home Guard, Auxiliary and Women's Services in the town.

Precautions had to be taken in case of air raids and the audience informed when the sirens had sounded the warning. This was done with a slide projected over the picture on the screen which, by recollection of an elderly patron informed me that it read '*An air raid has sounded. The show will continue and patrons may remain should they wish*'. Many did so though the practice nearly caused a possible tragedy just after Christmas 1940.

For most of the duration of the conflict the Oak Room Café was used as a canteen for the the workers of the factory next door to the cinema (now NHS Trust building on the site). Its use as a silver service restaurant was not possible but it still functioned as a café. One might even imagine a 'Workers Playtime', a popular daily radio show, being broadcast from there at least once during the War.

The Picture House was not the only place where films could be seen. Apart from casual shows in halls in the town using 16 mm equipment there were frequent visits to the town of a Ministry of Information Mobile Cinema. These were large pantechnicons fitted out with 16 mm or 35 mm portable projectors. Opening the rear doors would reveal a translucent screen shielded from the light by the doors and large retractable flaps. The films were shown by either direct rear projection or via a prism. These mobile cinemas were used to bring important wartime messages to the population such as how to cope with wartime conditions, preparation of food, hygiene and health etc. A favourite featured Tommy Trinder, a radio and screen comedy star, with a bouncing ball encouraging people to save for Victory by using the National Savings Scheme. These and similar shorts would be also shown on the Picture house screen in the twice-weekly programmes.

Exactly where these cinema vans set up in the town is not known but they would usually be found in central areas such as railway stations, town squares, parks and outside factories and the like.

By far the most important and tragic event for the cinema was the air raid of Saturday, 4 January 1941. The main feature showing that night was 'Rio' (1939) which starred Basil Rathbone, Victor McLaglen and Robert Cummins, Leo Carrillo and Billy Gilbert.

It was a programmer with a mixture of adventure and romance and because of the popular star line-up the house was full most of the day. The feature was nearing the end of the final reel due to the cinema having to close by 10 pm.

At around 9.40 pm or so the droning sound of a German bomber was heard over the town and a stick of bombs, six was reported, fell across the town at intervals

The shrapnel damage sustained in the 1941 bombing. Still visible today. *Authors collection*

A wartime cinema van. There were also larger cinema vans fitted out in furniture pantechnicans. *Courtesy of Charles Morris, Morris Northern Cinemas Ltd*

between Wellington Terrace and Binding & Payne's garage in Old Church Road. The fifth bomb landed at the bottom of Hillside Road opposite the entrance to the Picture House where it fractured a gas main. The damage was extensive. It blew off the roof of St John's School and all of the windows in the school were devastated. The front of the cinema was also extensively damaged with the doors of the Western entrance blown in and all the glass in the shops and the stained glass windows of the Oak Room totally destroyed which included the Lunette window above the entrance causing devastation in the Oak Room Lounge. Shrapnel pitted the stone-work over the entrance, the scars of which can still be clearly seen today.

The film was stopped as the bomb had also cut off all the power to the street. People sitting the balcony were reported to have said that they felt the whole of the balcony lift with the force of the explosion. The cinema was evacuated by the rear exits and none of the patrons or staff were injured by the explosion.

That cannot be said of the incident as a whole because in addition to some residents in the road two people had been standing by the entrance of the Picture House as the bomb fell. It is not known why they were there perhaps waiting for someone to come out of the cinema or just sheltering but the blast severely injured Private William Raith, 22, of Rotherham serving in the 4th Battalion of the East Yorkshire Regiment stationed nearby. He died a few hours later in hospital. He was buried in Clevedon Cemetery his grave looked after by the Commonwealth War Graves Commission.

The second person was Basil Sainsbury who came from Hull. Although injured by the blast he recovered.

The local newspaper report a few days later mentioned that in a raid over the Bristol Channel bombs fell on a town in the West. One bomb exploded near a picture house and there were a few casualties. Such was the restrictions on newspaper reporting in those days. Regardless of this report there are others who tell of another bomb falling, but not exploding, in the Coleridge Vale area. It was eventually removed by prisoners of War held in a camp nearby. Nice touch that.

The damage was repaired quickly and the cinema was operating again within a couple of days. The shop windows were boarded up with small windows to see through. Temporary repairs were made to the cinema and full restoration was completed in 1944 when building restrictions were eased to repair war damage in the country. The result of that is what you see today and the Lunette window over the west end of the cinema was never replaced.

There have been conflicting reports as to what happened on that night. In 1985 the account of the bomb incident was the subject of a feature in the local paper. A correspondent wrote to say that he was in the cinema that night and the usual air raid warning was flashed on the screen. The programme ended and several people walked along to Webb's fish and chip shop and whilst waiting to be served a loud explosion was heard. The shop lights went out and then came on again. It was not until the next day, the correspondent said, that he heard about the bomb and that a soldier had been killed in the doorway of the cinema by shrapnel.

The incident seems to attract conjecture but most accounts support the original version. In those days the cinema was on continuous performance and one would generally leave when having reached the point in the programme where one had gone in so perhaps that might be an explanation for the correspondent's view.

The final interest of note from the War years concerns an entry in the war diary of Lady Elton (Sir Ambrose's wife Dorothy Wiggin) which tells of Christmas time in 1945.

December 25th. 1945

We have very bad films here. The other day some Italian prisoners of War expressed their feelings about this whereby some of our soldiers did not like the colour of their hair and there was a bloody battle outside the Picture House.

During the years of conflict the Picture House continued to provide entertainment to alleviate an ever growing weariness of War, itself becoming a victim of it, but on Victory day it was proudly decorated in celebration.

9. The Maxime and the Curzon

The War years had, like most cinemas, been busy times for the Picture House. It was well worn so to speak and the same could be said for Victor Cox who had already had his family home, an exotic looking creation, built at the top of the Zig Zag in Clevedon and he was ready to move into other pastimes. By now he was the sole owner of the Clevedon Cinephone Company and therefore the Picture House. He put the cinema business on the market and it was bought by Maximillian Corne on the 11 June 1945.

Corne is said to have had other cinemas in the South-west. At around that time there was a cinema at Glastonbury, originally the Cinema or the Town Hall Cinema, which had been purchased and re-named the Maxime. Likewise in Street, Somerset there was a cinema called the Playhouse which changed hands a couple of times and in the late 1940s it also changed ownership and renamed Maxime.

Both of these cinemas are recorded as changing to the ownership of Cornell Cinemas (Sketty) Ltd. of Cardiff either during or immediately after WW2. Whilst there is no specific evidence in the fact that whilst the name Maxime was established at three cinemas in the South-west, each having changed

The "MAXIME" Cinema

Tel. 2158   **CLEVEDON**   Tel. 2158

Offers Superb Entertainment in an Ideal Atmosphere

MAKE THE "MAXIME" YOUR RENDEZVOUS

CONTINUOUS MONDAY and SATURDAY from 2.0 approx.
TUESDAY, WEDNESDAY, THURSDAY and FRIDAY
from 5.0 approx.   Prices 3s. 1d., 2s. 7d., 1s. 6d.
Children 14 years old and under reduced prices only if accompanied by adults

SEND YOUR BOY—SEND YOUR GIRL TO
THE MAXIME CINEMA CLUB
FOR BOYS AND GIRLS
MEETINGS EVERY SATURDAY MORNING — SPECIALLY
SELECTED FILMS, COMPETITIONS, TALKS, ETC.

Maxime publicity.

ownership at around the same time, it might be more than just a co-incidence that Corne, with Cardiff connections, having bought the Picture House at Clevedon had indeed added the cinema to a small chain with the Maxime branding.

Maximillian Corne was a portly and pleasant fellow. He was an entrepreneur and showman and he brought changes to the Picture House the most important one being on the 5 August 1946 when he changed the name of the cinema to the Maxime. This was rather an unusual name for the Clevedon cinema and it is thought that it was an amalgam or play on his own name. There were, however, more changes to come some of which do not readily have logistical reason and for the first time since 1922 the cinema was to see structural changes.

Corne had ideas to transform the cinema internally into a multi-facet building. Plans were drawn up for the stalls area to become a 'market hall' and dance hall but they never came to fruition. A 'plan' for such a conversion for the stalls area is thought to exist but gives no detailed information and one wonders what type of seating was envisaged or where it would have been stored when the 'hall' was not on cinema or indeed if the Stalls would even exist at all. Similar ideas were revived later in the cinema's history (see the Curzon chapter).

To accommodate these plans Corne intended to re-model the Balcony area by removing the loge seated area and building a projection room at the rear. The rear entrance to the Balcony was blocked in and a new entrance created utilising the circulation area leading to the Balcony toilets. It is also thought that at this time the boxes may have been blocked off and the balustrades fronting them removed. There is however more evidence that this was done in 1956 a view that I tend to respect.

That the projection room was moved to a new location at the rear of the Balcony and the original one turned into a storeroom and office I consider actually happened the evidence being that it would appear people remember it as so. Corne's plans to change the use of the cinema however seems to have come to nothing and as a result the Maxime continued much as before.

He did, however, revive some earlier features one being the very popular Saturday morning Children's matinees. It was publicised as the 'Maxime Cinema Club' and he encouraged parents to '*send their boy – send their girl along every Saturday morning to see specially selected films, enjoy competitions and talks etc*'.

I can't imagine talks being much appreciated in a children's cinema club in those days but records show that the cinema club was very popular.

The cinema programmes were printed monthly as they were in the Picture House days and extolled the cinema as offering *superb entertainment in an ideal atmosphere*. Two such programmes have come to light though both are only facsimiles. One dating from 1948 shows performances were continuous daily Monday to Saturday from 2 pm which of course meant that the showings went right through until closure at around 10.30 pm or later This would almost certainly consist of the feature, news and trailers being shown three times daily and the second feature twice with a last complete performance starting around 7.30 pm.

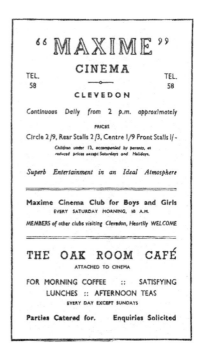

"MAXIME"

CINEMA

TEL. 58 —o— TEL. 58

CLEVEDON

Continuous Daily from 2 p.m. approximately

PRICES

Circle 2/9, Rear Stalls 2/3, Centre 1/9 Front Stalls 1/-

Children under 12, accompanied by parents, at reduced prices except Saturdays and Holidays.

Superb Entertainment in an Ideal Atmosphere

Maxime Cinema Club for Boys and Girls
EVERY SATURDAY MORNING, 10 A.M.

MEMBERS of other clubs visiting Clevedon, Heartily WELCOME

THE OAK ROOM CAFÉ
ATTACHED TO CINEMA

FOR MORNING COFFEE :: SATISFYING LUNCHES :: AFTERNOON TEAS
EVERY DAY EXCEPT SUNDAYS

Parties Catered for.   Enquiries Solicited

The prices at that time were Circle 2/9d. (note that balcony had now become the circle), Rear Stalls 2/3d., Centre Stalls 1/9d. and Front Stalls 1/-, the benches having been long past replaced with cinema seats.

The second is for 1953, which may have been at the take over by new owners, when the performance times have changed to continuous Monday and Saturday from 2 pm and from 5 pm Tuesday to Friday where the main feature, news and the trailers were shown twice and the second feature once. The oddity is the prices being 3/1d., presumed for the Circle, 2/7d. for the Rear Stalls and 1/6d. Front Stalls. These peculiar prices, however, reflect the entertainment tax levied on cinemas in those days. It is also interesting to note that children under 12 had to be accompanied by an adult if they wanted to enjoy a reduced price for entry. Now why don't we do that today? Interesting too is the rear panel of the programme advertising the Oak Room Café.

Always a useful way of finding cinema ownership is to read through the Kinematograph Year Books which were produced until latter years. The entries

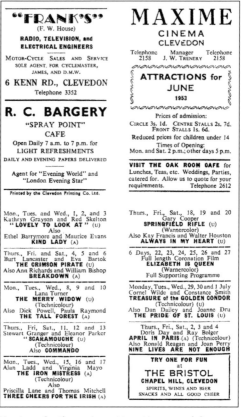

Maxime forthcoming attractions card for June 1953

would tell you who owned the cinema, seating, prices of admission and some technical information. They can be useful but sometimes wholly inaccurate for the stated year as it was up to each cinema to inform of any changes, and many did not.

For the year 1945 the cinema was still listed as the Picture House with ownership by the Clevedon Cinephone Company with Victor Cox as the Proprietor and Manager. For the year 1947 it stated that the Governing Director was Maximillian Corne but still in the Company name of Clevedon Cinephone Company. Film bookings for the Maxime were undertaken at Ocean Chambers, Dumfries Place, Cardiff, and in 1948 at St Johns Square in Cardiff. This is interesting because for the first time there seems is evidence of a connection with the Welsh capital and Corne.

For most of the time the manager of the Maxime was Mr Trenory. He was very popular with the patrons and quite a character in his own right and becoming a firm favourite with the children attending the Saturday morning Cinema Club.

It is also known that around this time, or probably a little later, the cinema suffered a problem when necessary work to the course of the river that runs by the building caused some interference with the cinema's foundations. Deep cracks were caused in the lower flooring and this in turn affected the outer walls and the Balcony which was 'hung' on the rear wall and the side- walls. Remedial work was put in place and evidence of that can be seen both in the uneven level of the floor in the original part of the building dating back to 1912 and more apparent by the ties which render support for the two great outer walls part of which can still be seen in the auditorium today. It was the time probably that the two balcony support pillars were put in place cemented into large buttresses below the auditorium and extensive steelwork on the underside of the balcony though this may have been done in a lengthy closure in 1956.

Changes were however afoot yet again. In 1953 it seems that Maximillian Corne sold the cinema, and business. The reason is not listed as far as can be determined. Around the same time the Glastonbury Maxime closed, it deemed being unsuitable for the installation of Cinemascope and the Street Maxime was sold to Myles Byrne Cinemas.

Strange that three cinemas in the region with the same name were sold at around the same time. So it *is* possible Corne could have been involved with all three.

In 1953 the cinema business was still pretty buoyant although the increase in television broadcasting and the arrival of colour TV was making inroads into peoples leisure pursuits. Cinema retaliated with a wider screen format, 3-D and Cinemascope with Stereophonic sound, all of which the minuscule TV screen could not emulate.

Some of the more robust circuits such as Rank, ABC, Granada and Essoldo were buying up independent houses renovating and re-equipping them with the latest cinema technology. For many however these technological improvements were impossible and eventually closed for the same reasons that closed the Maxime at Glastonbury.

Whilst a number smaller circuits closed at that time some expanded and one such company was the Cleeve Cinema Company of 9 Windsor Place, Cardiff. This company had a number of cinemas in Wales and the South-west one being the

Forum at Bath until around 1934. (At that time it was associated with the Avon Cinema Company though based in Cardiff.)

In August 1953 the Cleeve Cinema Company bought out the Clevedon Cinephone Company and took over the Maxime as a going concern.

Technical

For the major part of the time as the Maxime the equipment was:

2 BTH Argons were installed along with BTH Carbon Arc lamps.
The sound system was changed to BTH.
The speaker system was still housed in a Roxy cabinet. The speakers in the installation were GB Duosonic with a GB high frequency horn mounted on the cabinet to 'spread' the sound.

The projection room of the Maxime *circa* 1955 shortly before up-grade to Widescreen and Cinemascope. *Courtesy of W.G. Griffin*

The CURZON

Little change seems to have taken place with the take-over by the Cleeve Cinema Company of Cardiff. A small circuit with cinemas mainly in Wales the Company had three directors. Wyndham Lewis, P. Norman-Wright and J. Wyndham Lewis, Wyndham's son. On take-over the operation of the Maxime remained and the cinema continued as before. The Kinematograph Year Book for 1954 recorded that Clevedon's population was 14,000 and that the Maxime had 815 seats priced between 1s. 6d. and 3s. 1d. The performances were continuous with two changes of programme weekly and the film programmes booked at the head office in Cardiff. The cinema was still listed as having a café.

Cinema, still facing the increase in TV ownership, had introduced the new innovations of Widescreen, 3-Dimension and Cinemascope to woo the public back into the cinema and in many places achieved success. Films themselves had progressed too with the technical advances being made. More colour, stereophonic sound with the new screen formats and the super cinemas that were large enough and belonging to major circuits were once again in business.

Many smaller independents, and some smaller circuit houses who could accommodate the new screens and sound technology also re-equipped to enjoy many more years of life.

Others could not accommodate the new screens being conversions from other buildings or from lack of space and gave up. Closure of the Portishead cinema being a case in question which I write about later.

The Maxime continued much as before with its policy of family entertainment on its traditional screen. Widescreen, as opposed to the Academy shape, may have been shown with some adaptation of lenses and picture aperture and as always the films shown were quite a long period after their release nationally. Much of the programming was still dominantly British films and with an abundance of good British product in the late 40s and the 50s audiences remained loyal though with car purchase becoming popular and there still being good public transport locally many people saw the latest films from Hollywood in Bristol long before the Maxime had them.

On the 10 March 1956 the cinema closed as the Maxime. During the seven weeks of closure the cinema underwent alterations and the installation of a Cinemascope screen some 25ft wide and 16ft high (approximately). This gave a picture size of around 23ft x 15ft To ensure the maximum size of screen could

The Curzon. Top: This picture was taken after the alterations of 1956.
Below: A recent picture *Authors collection*

be installed and to allow for the speakers to be installed behind the screen the new tubular screen frame was brought forward to about half-way down stage. There was no installation to up-grade the sound system however. To ensure reasonable sight lines in the Balcony the screen had to be tilted considerably resulting in a lesser viewing quality in the front of the stalls. That may have resulted in the removal of seats from the front at that time and not later for Bingo as reported.

I referred earlier to alterations in the auditorium, mainly the boxes being sealed off and balustrades removed. There is some controversy as to when that happened but I think that it was likely it took place within this period of closure. The second projection room (if not already in place) was created at the rear of the balcony using the space occupied by seating.

A redecoration took place and the base colour on the walls and proscenium became fawn and gold relief-work completely obliterated. Buttresses were painted pink and the in-filling of the boxes were covered in red wallpaper with black and white motifs. Balcony rails were brown. The walls below the old boxes and the balcony front were in cream. In the stalls dado rails and below were dark grey. The edge of the proscenium arch and the pediment relief was gold.

Seating seems to have remained as before. If, and when, the seating and other furnishings were changed over the preceding years is obscure but the remanents found today in the disused balcony suggest that some seats, made by Kalee, had brown plush upholstery. The carpeting is also brown as is the upholstered balcony edge. It must be assumed with some certainty that the stalls were furnished similarly

The cinema re-opened on the 30 April1956 under its new name **Curzon** with the war adventure film 'Cockleshell Heroes' (1955) a Cinemascope picture which starred Jose Ferrer, Trevor Howard (a popular British star), Dora Bryan and Anthony Newly. It is interesting to note that the newly named cinema continued the tradition of exhibiting home film product as opposed to the many excellent Hollywood films around at the time that were filmed in the wide screen process although, as usual, it was a year after the film's release nationally.

Programmes were continuous from 5.30 pm and from 2.30 pm on Tuesdays and Saturdays. Prices were Stalls 1/6d. and 2/3d. Circle 2/9d. with the Grand Circle (one row at the front of the circle with plenty of leg room and best seats) priced at 3/2d. Total seating in the cinema was 787.

Sunday showing as a regular pattern was introduced soon after. The first show was on Sunday, 6 May, 1956 with the screening of 'Privates Progress' (1956)

starring Ian Carmichael, Terry Thomas and Richard Attenborough. Interesting to note that this film was relatively new – a significant change from tradition. No children were allowed to Sunday performances, however, regardless of the film's certificate.

So the cinema settled down under its new name and a new screen and battled through the many years to come competing with TV and later video. Bingo was introduced at some stage and recorded as being on Sunday night so obviously the Sunday night films were not well attended In 1968 the cinema put on more Bingo with sessions on Sunday, Monday, Tuesday and Wednesday evenings. To accommodate the Bingo gaming machines some seats were removed from the front of the stalls reducing the total seating for the cinema to 708.

A few other notable and interesting items took place during this period. In 1955 plans were submitted to remove the boxes which does tend to prove this happened at the time of the 1956 closure. On 6 April 1959 plans were deposited with the Clerk to the Justices at Flax Bourton for a new Dance Floor. This rather suggests that there were previous plans for a Dance floor or that one actually existed?. The plans were submitted by builders T.H. Oakley of Cumberland Grove, Bristol and by John Topham, AMI Municipal engineers to the Clevedon Urban DistrictCouncil, for planning permission.

In 1962 plans were submitted, this time in a letter, sent again to the Clerk of Justices, supporting plans for a Market Hall in the stalls area. The letter concerned asking for permission to build a concrete raft over the stalls to construct a new floor and other alterations for the creation a cinema to seat 300 people in the Balcony area. What happened to the plans is unknown. The stalls were never converted so possibly the plans were refused or abandoned. 1962 also saw yet more plans this time to remove the projection room from its position behind the circle to its original one at the rear of the stalls. Again the plans were not taken forward. Like-wise in 1971 the cinema apparently closed for three days from Monday to Wednesday 15–17 May but no reason was given for this closure though it may have been to install projection equipment. On the following day, 18 May, the Curzon re-opened with 'Cromwell' (1970) starring Richard Harris and Alec Guinness.

An interesting programme for the week on 1 January 1965 was advertising 'From Russia With Love' (1963) two years after release – the second 007 picture with Sean Connery. Announced also was Bingo every Thursday at 8 pm price 2/6d. 20 games 3/- The cinema was apparently closed on Sundays.

Through the sixties and into the seventies the Curzon continued to provide a diet of pictures and bingo. In Chapter 11 we will meet some of the people who visited

The Curzon auditorium following alterations and closure of the the Balcony. *Authors collection*

The Curzon auditorium 1997. *Authors collection*

and worked there but another great change to the building, now fifty years old, came on the 9 March 1973 when it was advertised that the Curzon would close after the last show on Saturday 24 March at the end of a three day run of 'Cabaret' (1972) for extensive alterations.

Not since the Fifties were alterations of such intensity made to the cinema. The plans to return the projection room to its original position behind the stalls were revived and undertaken. The Balcony was taken out of use and a false ceiling was fitted from the edge of the balcony to part way down the proscenium obscuring from view the barrel-vaulted ceiling, proscenium arch and making redundant the upper toilets, balcony lounge and cloakrooms and gallery areas. This also rendered the exits to the lower floor on the Actors left side of the building defunct and also access to the fly gallery and dressings rooms, though these were long past disused.

Changes to the lower floors were also made. The screen end of the auditorium was greatly changed with new exits being created and alterations made to the stage. It was at this time also that the whole of the stalls area panelling was covered by a decorative fabric which not only gave the hall more cosy appearance but improved the sound quality also. The eastern entrance was blocked off creating another shop unit and the Oak room closed off from the cinema by giving it a separate entrance. The rear exits were altered also. It is believed there were some seating changes and with the closure of the circle and remodelling of the stalls the total seating was reduced to around 400. There were other alterations. Most notable was the western entrance and foyer being divided the outer segment becoming yet another shop unit. The box office was removed to the side of the entrance below the steps up to the auditorium. One observer likened the appearance of the new entrance to the cinema from the road as having a distinctive look of a 'dubious side-show'.

The original 1920s projection room at stalls level was extended into the auditorium, necessary with more modern and bulky projection equipment requiring a better working environment.

There was another re-decoration. Now that the walls were covered in the orange fabric everything else became orange also including the doors, front of the projection room wall and the reduced foyer area with red being the other colour used . Below the orange material the dado and skirting were done out in what can best be described as a dull maroon. It is thought that at this time the blue carpet was fitted and blue upholstered seats installed though this cannot be truly established. Frankly it was ghastly.

The upper projection room after removal of projection equipment to the original room in 1973. This room now houses part of the Curzon Collection of heritage projection equipment. *Authors collection*

The 'timetable' for the last programme to be shown from the upper projection room in 1973. *Authors collection*

The Curzon re-opened on Thursday, 19 April 1973 with Bingo with films starting the following day. However, the first film advertisement to be found was for the following week, Friday, 27 April 1973, being Walt Disney's 'Robin Hood' (1973) which seemed to herald a new booking system, carried out from head office in Cardiff, with more recent films with less emphasis on British products. Shows were continuous on Fridays from 5.30 pm and Saturdays from 2.00 pm The prices were in the new currency at 30p Adult, Children and OAPs at 25p – can you imagine going to the pictures for 30p (6/-).

Until 1980 the cinema continued much as before. In that year another significant change was made when, obviously for economy reasons, the cinema projection system was singled utilising a long-play film feed system removing the need to employ two projectors for presentation (and likely projectionists). It seems that from that time also the cinema reverted to seven day running of films, bingo ceasing to be operated. At that time also the operation became a once nightly performance starting around 5.30pm, or later depending upon the length of the programme, and consisting of a main feature film and a short or two features. One such programme was 'Coal Miners Daughter' (1980) and 'Fame' (1980) both over 2 hours long all for the price of £1.30. Nearly five hours of entertainment which was still good value.

Over the next few years, under the stewardship of the Eagles, Ken as the Chief Projectionist and Janet as the manager, the Cleeve Cinema Company kept the Curzon going. When Wyndham Lewis, the proprietor passed away the Company was taken over by his son J. Wyndham Lewis. It seems that unlike the father, a well liked man by his employees, who looked after the business, his son did not having other business interests which we will not go into. Left very much to their own devices the Eagles kept the Curzon operating, though it must be said that without the support the owner should have given them, they struggled and inevitably the cinema suffered.

The problem eventually came to a head in 1995 when the Cleeve Cinema Company was put into Receivership. Although the Curzon at Clevedon was still a going concern other cinemas in the chain, by this time only one, had all suffered from lack of investment and modernisation which in turn resulted in loss of business and closed.

The final chapter of the Curzon could have taken place in 1995 but for the nerve and fortitude of a small group of people who were about to turn the ailing cinema on its head.

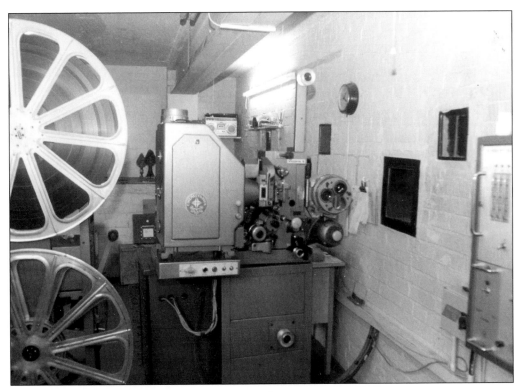

The Curzon projection room in 1997. *Authors collection*

Technical

When the Cleeve Cinema Company took over in 1953 they inherited the projection equipment *in situ*. They were 2 BTH Argon Projectors, BTH Arc Lamps and GB Dousonic sound system.

By 1960 however the BTH projectors had been replaced with Kalee 12s, Kalee President Arc Lamps and Westrex Sound. Certainly the higher powered arc lamps would have been essential with the installation of Cinemascope. The Kalee 12s were themselves replaced by Kalee 21s these projectors retaining the excellent President carbon arc lamps.

In 1980 there was a complete change of projection equipment. The White Palace at Pontypridd, had closed and the projection equipment removed to the Curzon. The White Palace was on a single system of projection using a Cinemeccanica Victoria 5 with a Cinemeccanica 1600 watt Zenon lamp. Tower continuous film feed and sound system P100 (mono) by the same manufacturer. The equipment was installed as new in the White Palace in 1970 and transferred on closure to the Curzon. To where the Kalee 21s were disposed is not known.

The sound system was not changed when the Cinemascope installation was carried out.

Cinemascope optical was produced, as basic three channels of sound and an ambient channel for the effects track. It was never used in that way. The Roxy Box (on take-over in 1996) was still situated behind the screen centrally with the same speaker arrangement. There were no LH or RH speaker cabinets nor any ambient units in the auditorium. The sound, strictly monaural, was reproduced apparently in a 'mixed' form which is presumably what the audience heard.

The western end of the cinema as it is today. The attractive brickwork is a feature of both ends of the cinema. The sign for taxis denotes there was a cab stand by the cinema before Great Western road was laid. Exposed now the western wall cries out for the removal of intrusive signs then cleaned and floodlit. *Courtesy of Jon Webber*

The present foyer opened up again from a shop unit. *Author collection*

Refurbished entrance
to the auditorium.
Author collection

The eastern wall of the Curzon as it is today with the exterior of Type's coach house very much as it was. The old balcony exit can still be recognised by the recess next to the left-hand door. *Courtesy of Jon Webber*

Another view of the cinema. The words 'Picture House' can just be picked out below the window. Should this be saved before it fades away altogether? It has been there for over 80 years. *Origin unknown*

10. Curzon Community Cinema

News of the taking into Administrative Receivership of the Cleeve Cinema Company was reported in the Clevedon Mercury in July 1995. It was an unexpected shock to the populace of Clevedon and the surrounding communities. Their local cinema seemed doomed to follow the path of so many others. The problem seemed to be that since the death of Wyndham Lewis senior a few years earlier the business had been in some turmoil financially, though it has to be said the Curzon still remained a going concern mostly because of the efforts of both Janet and Kenneth Eagles and a loyal staff. Regardless of that the circuit, which now only comprised of the Curzon at Clevedon and the cinema at Haverford West which the Company ran on a 'tenant' basis for the Local Authority, the Cleeve Cinema Company was bankrupt.

Jon Webber on arriving home after a holiday was browsing through the accumulated newspapers which had been pushed through his letter-box whilst he was away came upon the announcement in the 'Mercury' and became immediately 'galvanised' declaring to all asunder that *the cinema is to close? Not likely'*. Jon had good cause to make this claim. In the late seventies he had been involved with the 'saving and development' of the Rio Cinema at Dalston, London. As a Community Development worker he successfully led a campaign to purchase the Rio and operate it as a Community business which was successful and is still open as a cinema today.

Using this experience and knowledge he gathered a few like minded people together and put forward the possibility of doing something on a community basis to save the Curzon.

A public meeting was called at the Curzon to which 700 people attended to listen to his plans to keep the cinema running. The cost of purchase was £200,000 and a buyer, a local Church group, were in the market. So began a year of campaigning gaining support in the form of loans, donations and business plans and with those attending the original meeting pledging money in the knowledge that the Receivers were willing to continue to administrate the cinema thereby keeping the Curzon open whilst all this was going on.

The plan was to create a community business called The Curzon-Clevedon Community Centre for the Arts and to be formally established as a Company Limited by Guarantee. It was registered with Companies House as a Limited Company with limited liability for its members of £1 and was to trade as a not-for-profit organization, any profits generated being re-invested in the cinema and other community activities.

At the same time a National banking concern was brought on board on a 'community prestige' platform and by the latter part of 1996 the enterprise was ready to purchase the cinema from the Receivers on a raft of proposals which met their requirements. At this time it was learned that a campaign to have the cinema building listed as Grade 2, essentially safeguarding its use as a cinema, had been successful.

On 26 November 1996, and without any closure, the Curzon became the CURZON COMMUNITY CINEMA and the longevity of cinema on the site was maintained.

On the 'opening night' the British film 'Brassed Off' (1966) starring Pete Posstlethwaite and Ewan McGregor was shown continuing the old Picture House tradition of showing British films and there were speeches. The Clevedon Town Band gave a short concert of music from the film.

The cinema runs on part paid and part voluntary staffing which allows costs to be kept as low as possible. Since 1996 improvements to the run-down cinema have taken place with, on the technical side, a new screen and masking being installed – you should have seen the state of the old one having been *in situ* since 1956. A new sound system installed which, at the time of writing, is the very latest and more up to date than many multiplex sites. As I write the original west-end entrance foyer has been opened up and the seating has been re-furbished.

There are ambitions plans to restore the cinema, as far as that is possible bearing in mind the need to provide the best and latest in cinema comfort and technology. In the years that have passed much has been achieved but there is much more to do. The cinema suffers from highs and lows in occupancy and at times, if operated purely commercially, would have failed. The fabric of the building is showing its eighty-two years of use and particularly because little has been spent on it throughout its longevity. It has not failed and that is due to the enthusiasm of a few people and the many volunteers and supporting patrons who go to the pictures regularly – to the Curzon Picture House that is.

Technical

At the end of 2003 the Cinemeccanica Victoria 5 is still in use and is now thirty-three years old and still going strong. On take over the light source was a Cinemeccanica 1650 watt Zenon as fitted in 1980. The screen was the original Cinemascope installed in 1956.

The light source was upgraded to a Cinemeccanica Zenith 2000X but with a 2500 lamp running well as basic. There are plans to further increase the light output with a 4000 watt installation. The old screen has been replaced with a new one which has new acoustical masking. Up-grading of the projection lenses also improved the picture.

The sound system on take-over in 1996 was a Cinemeccanica monaural P100 with a Roxy box centre stage behind the screen utilising GB lower and mid-range speakers and a 'tweeter' horn assembly atop.

In 1998 this was changed to an interim sound system arrangement utilising a Phillips De-coder 'home cinema' unit able to separate the stereo channels thus providing a 'surround sound' for the auditorium. This was installed primarily to improve the sound for screening of blockbuster films, 'Titanic' being the first to receive the system. Two additional speakers were installed behind the screen to provide separate channels utilising the Roxy box for the centre channel. Small ambient speakers were installed in the auditorium. It worked very well but after five years of use it was failing so a decision was taken to go all the way and install full Dolby Digital Ex Sound.

At the time of writing the Curzon sound installation comprises the following:

Dolby Digital red-light sound head
Dolby CP650 Digital Cinema Sound Processor
Dolby CM60 Six Channel Monitor
Technics SL P63 CD (digital option) player unit
Rane MLM 82a Mixer
Martin Model 112, 2 Channel infra-red hearing assistance system
Martin CMX 14 Cinema controller
6 QSC RMX 1450 Power Amplifiers
Dolby Screentalk and Audio Description.

Additional equipment includes Eikie model LC-X1100 DVD/Video Cassette Projector and Eikie EX 3000 16 mm Projector.

The western end of the cinema in 2000. *Courtesy of Jon Webber*

The auditorium 2004 the original panelling still intact.

The original panelling revealed.

The Curzon projection room 2004.

The Dolby digital sound system 2004.

A new screen goes up. Replacement of the screen in 2001.

All authors collection

11. People, Events – Life and Legends

With the historical background of the previous chapters firmly in our minds what of the life of this cinema phenomenon rapidly, as I write, reaching a centenary. It is not, however, just a building. Cinemas have a life created by the people who work in them and this helps to give the cinema its place in the community. Perhaps it is best to trace some of this by looking at some of the people and tales about the Picture House, The Maxime and the Curzon as each has its own place in the way of things.

Victor Cox and The Picture House

Part of Victor Cox's earlier life was illustrated within an early chapter of this book but why and how did he start in the cinema business with his father James Newton Cox instead of following him into the family business. By all accounts the Cox's were 'very reserved' It is said that 'old Mr Cox's, I take that to be Victor's Grandfather, was a German by descent and behaved like a 'Prussian King' and in the First World War he would to go to the highest point in Clevedon and signal to German aircraft. I find this somewhat beguiling as according to Church Registers of the time it is recorded that when James Newton was first married he was, as expected, single and a stonemason, living and working in Clevedon his father being a hotel manager by profession. What of Victor and what was he like?

Without a doubt cinema in Clevedon owes its existence to Victor Cox. He was a well respected man who seem in latter years to have a certain amount of power in the Town.

He maintained an efficiently run House and was apparently liked by his staff. This did not say however that he was an easy man to get on with. As far as the cinema was concerned he liked his own way and things were done accordingly. He was erudite and hard headed as far as the business was concerned and expected everyone else to be so minded.

He would not spend a pound when a penny would do. George Diamond, who worked at the cinema as a Button boy in the 1930s, remembers being called out to work extra time on a Saturday. Victor had gone to his house personally to fetch him. He remembers working all day for the same pay as if he had worked his shift only. Victor's stepmother worked with him in the cinema and both were found either in the two pay boxes, playing the piano or singing for the silent films. When the talkies came Victor was still in evidence around the cinema keeping an eye on things himself and little boys who didn't behave as he expected.

We have already learned that Victor was fascinated with the new fangled moving pictures whilst he was in college at South Kensington and whilst on a vacation in 1910 he joined with his father to run a series of 'living pictures' in the Public Hall. Quite whether he left college at that time or no he was to stake all of his small amount of capital and a tremendous amount of energy into building the first Picture House on land held by his father. Later he was entirely responsible for the re-build in 1920. The present building.

Victor still found time to assist his father in the Monumental Masons business and after his father's death in 1932 and selling the cinema in 1945 he took on the business fully until 1968. Stone and wood carvings by Victor are still evident in various parts of the town and district. He also commissioned a controversial style of house on Dial Hill which he called 'Sunway' which is still visible today high on the hill. In his later years he turned his attention to an almost unlimited energy to benefit Clevedon working for the Community Centre and membership of Rotary as well as leaving an endowment towards an eventual Clevedon Museum amongst many other benefits.

Victor died aged 90 in June 1978. The Picture House and now the Curzon was Victor's cinema. He built it, he ran it to a high standard and to this day it serves as a fitting memorial to him.

Stan Newton 'Stan the camera man'

Stan Newton was a projectionist, one could say THE projectionist throughout a large part of the life of Clevedon's cinema. Stanley was born in 1895 and the son of John Newton, a Mason and living at Battery Cottages, Clevedon. He was the third of six children although two elder brothers died in infancy. It is thought that John Newton must have worked at the Cox's masonry business for two reasons.

First, although perhaps co-incidental, names in both families were similar and perhaps not co-incidentally Stanley went to work for Victor Cox at the first Picture House.

He started at the Picture House by all accounts in 1912 as a 'Chocolate Boy' which by its title indicates that he took confectionery around the cinema during intervals between the films. By the age of 20 he was a projector operator at the cinema. He married Elizabeth Jane Colenso in

Stanley Newton. 'Stan the camera-man' at work in the Maxime projection room. *Courtesy of the Projected Picture Trust*

1918 his wife's father recorded as being a Miner. He spent all of his working life as a projectionist and by the time of his retirement in 1966 had worked 55 years at the same cinema, a record for the industry by any stretch of the imagination and certainly for the South-west.

He was to become known as 'Stan the Cameraman'. Why exactly is a puzzlement as he was at the other end of the profession but in those days projectors were regarded by some as a camera, perhaps a reference to the early days of cinematography when the camera was also a printer and projector (Lumiere Brothers Cinemematographe). He was well liked, cheerful and liked a joke. Donald Bishop who worked under him as an assistant deputy projectionist describes Stan as good Chief Projectionist who knew his job and was able to pass that expertise to all those who worked under him.

People who knew him at the time of his retirement relate that he happily professed to having little interest in the films he showed. He just liked projectors. He apparently only saw one film right through in his career and that was 'Sound of Music'. This must have been at the very end of his long projection career. He certainly was a progressive watching and being a part of the growth of the industry from the early silent films right through to sound and the latest technology of Cinemascope. Sadly he has gone to his cinema in the sky but I like to think that he would have approved of the knowledge that his old cinema still shows pictures and has a selection of a few of the old projectors he probably used in its heritage Collection.

There have been many other people who have worked at the cinema during the years and it is only possible to make a brief reference in this book to a few of those mentioned to me.

Donald Bishop was a projectionist and later in the 1950s Assistant Chief Projectionist. During the Curzon days Bill Butland worked as a projectionist and later was Manager. His wife Lillian was Cashier and involved with management. There was a Mr Carroll who was also a Manager but the dates are obscure. Molly Coles was an Usherette and Molly Dawson was also an Usherette during the 1940s. George Diamond we have already met. He was a Button Boy and then an Usher in the Picture House days as was Usherette Mrs Green and a name from the days of the Maxime, Barbara Mole who was a Cashier. Peter Leveritt was a projectionist in the 1940s. and Peter went back to the cinema for his wedding reception in the Oak Room in 1951.

There are two people who still serve the cinema today both having been staff from the original Curzon. Margaret Keely remembers going to the old Picture House for the first time when she was five years old and the film she saw was

'Song of the South' (1946). At that time her family lived in Nailsea in a house cum shop opposite the old Glassworks site which had on the wall a publicity board advertising the films showing at the Picture House.

There was, however, one lady who must have a place in this book and that would be Mrs Green. An usherette for many years she is well remembered by Clevedonians particularly those who went to the cinema during their teens. She was a stickler and would have no nonsense. Should she catch those entering the cinema without paying she escort them outside without ceremony. In her days the cinema was on continuous performance which meant that you could go in around 5.30 pm and see the feature twice but not if Mrs Green saw you go in. A polite but firm reminder that your 'time was up' told anyone caught that they had overstayed their welcome. Another practice she undertook

Bill Butland, Manager and Lillian Butland, Cashier in the early Curzon days. The lady in the centre is a Mrs. White who is receiving a cheque for winning on the National bingo game, 1969
Courtesy of the Butland family.

was to separate the boys from the girls in the cinema whenever she could. Boys one side, girls the other. This did not last past the start of the big picture however. For all this Mrs Green was a kindly lady and much revered by picture-goers of Clevedon.

Going to the kid's matinees run by Max Corne was the highlight of the week. Getting to the cinema early meant getting to sit up in the Balcony (*surprising as generally the balconies were not used for children's shows for safety reasons*) and then spending their time waiting for the film to start by dropping empty ice cream cups on those in the stalls below and finally the mad rush for the exits before the National anthem was played (a habit that would continue well into adulthood).

A visit to the cinema on Saturday nights meant queuing along Old Church Road to get in to the early show with all the young people perched along the top of the wall bordereding the pavement in those days. There was always a rush to get a back row seat in the Balcony and although the picture size was smallish by today's standards it was adequate. Having said that not many couples on that back row were paying to much attention to what was on the screen by all accounts.

In the earlier days of the Curzon when business was slack serving sweets and ice cream was also part of the Cashiers job. Jeanette Maycock remembers those who were also at the Curzon in those days. Kathy Vincent helped out with the confectionery sales when times were busy and Carol Holmes worked as an usherette. Jeanette, working still as a Cashier, also has cause to remember elder Wyndham-Lewis who on one occasion made it his business to speak to her about a matter for which she was completely blameless. He was not too charming she recalls.

Commissionaires

Most cinemas in past days employed a Commissionaire, usually ex-servicemen. Dressed in a splendid uniform they were to be found at the entrance to the cinema. They were the bane of young lads who fancied their chances at getting in without paying and usually being foiled in the attempt if they came up against them but they were a much respected part of cinema-life marshalling the queue on a Saturday night touching the cap to regular patrons as they entered the cinema.

The cinema in Clevedon was no exception and I have discovered just two who dressed in a resplendent uniform stood stalwartly at the front of house. The Commissionaire at the rebuilt Picture House for many years was Jack Sims who also ran a taxi business, no doubt also being Commissionaire, to his advantage.

As his picture is in monochrome it is not possible to describe the colour and adornments but as the portrait shows he was a man of authority and commanded due respect to his position.

During the Second World War Bert Cutler filled the role for a time as having been wounded and invalided out of the Army Victor Cox gave him the job whilst he was undergoing a long rehabilitation. Margaret Keely, who is a relative to the Cutler family, remembers the uniform as being a large customary great coat maroon in colour with gold facings, epaulettes and brass buttons. He wore a smart peaked cap regally completing the outfit.

Today cinemas generally have a Chief of Staff who fulfil much of the work the Commissionaires undertook which included responsibility for all staff and duties front of house as well as keeping order.

Commissioaire Jack Sims 1929.
Source unknown

Whilst researching for this book I discovered one or two 'legends and myths' which are worth relating. I came across this description of a visit to the 'silent' Picture House for which I must thank Aubry Cook and the late Joan Birch. The account relates that a western was being shown and in one scene there were three old men sitting around a stove in a shack chewing tobacco and they would occasionally spit on the stove which sent loud hissing noises through the cinema. Now how did they reproduce that sound do you suppose?. Another account tells of the time Chaplin's 'The Gold Rush' was showing and there were queues around the block with the house packed to capacity. The scene where the wooden shack was being hurled along in the gale brought much activity in the cinema as the piano player increased the tempo to the sound effect of the howling wind. (just how that was achieved is also not recorded). The audience were exhilarated as they watched the shack wildly twisting and turning in the gale and ending up balanced on the edge of the precipice held from toppling over by a rope with a knot in it, caught between the rocks. Then suddenly there was silence from the pianist, audience suddenly hushed by the scene and only sound effect of the shrieking wind filling the auditorium. Suddenly the piano fires into life again when Chaplin triumphs over his adversity and the audience goes wild with applause.

As with many old buildings, especially cinemas and theatres, there is reputed to be a ghost in the cinema that emerges occasionally and then only on a Tuesday morning around 9.30am. This story was told to me a number of years ago and not entirely convinced about such an apparition I have found nothing to substantiate the story. I can remember having once been in the building around that time feeling decidedly uneasy about a clammy atmosphere pervading the remoter parts of the cinema which I could not readily dismiss. Is a spirit of the past, perhaps Victor Cox, keeping an eye on things? It is a good conversation piece when showing someone around the more remote parts of the old cinema building some of which can be quite un-nerving – and I can tell you from experience that the old building creaks and groans if you find yourself alone within it at late at night.

Publicity for the cinema in those days was done mainly by handbills delivered to shops and houses (some of them of the Public kind). A man was employed to accompany two or three boys who were paid a small fee to 'post' the leaflets ensuring that they were delivered however, the boys were up to this and rid themselves as quickly as possible of their bundle by depositing several leaflets in each house because the sooner they finished the sooner they received their payment and their complimentary ticket. One evening there was a group of such boys seated enjoying their earnings, part of which had been spent on a cigarette or two. As they sat acquiescently smoking Victor Cox came upon them whilst doing a spot check on tickets and all the lads had were a half price children's complimentary. Seeing this Victor turned to them and declared '*if you are young enough to get in with half-price tickets and then sit smoking you are old enough to pay full price. What is it to be?*' Unfortunately the result was not recorded. So inconsiderate was Victor Cox at times.

As I have recounted previously many well-known and famous people frequented the Picture House when visiting the town. One such person was George Bernard Shaw the famous playwright who for many years refused to allow film versions of his books and once said to Samuel Goldwyn '*the trouble is Mr Goldwyn you are interested in Art, whereas I am interested in money*'. He called at the cinema on an evening when he was in town and Blanche Harwood was in her usual place in the pay box at the 'posh' end. He arrived a little late and Blanche informed him that he had missed some of the main feature to which he replied '*Jolly good job too*' bought his ticket and went in.

During the building of the second Picture House there was an interesting event which shows how Victor Cox rewarded the hard work that had taken place to build the cinema.

It concerns an outing undertaken by staff and builders. I reproduce the article exactly as it was written so as to illustrate an example of the journalist reporting style of the time:

Clevedon Mercury: 3 September 1921

The large staff of workmen engaged in the construction and finishing work of Clevedon's new Picture House organised and enjoyable outing last week when a delightful tour was made of Cheddar, Wells, Glastonbury and other beauty spots in the neighbourhood. The journey was undertaken in two motor-coaches supplied by Messrs Binding and Payne. The party who were photographed by Mr. E. Hazel of Linden Road Studios was a thoroughly representative one and a striking feature was the happy spirit of comradeship displayed by all who took part. The organisers of the tour were pleased to have with them Mr. Victor Cox of the Picture House who, by the way, had carried out the building personally, from the beginning, without accident of any kind, and they were also favoured with the company of Mrs. Cox, wife of J.N. Cox and Mrs. Dean, the pianist, whilst J.N. Cox, although unable, to the regret of everyone, to make the journey, put in an appearance to give the tourists a hearty send off. Another absentee was the man behind the scenes or, in other words, the operator. (Assumed to be Stan Newton)

Many of the mechanics working on the building hail from Bristol, Taunton, Portishead, Cardiff and Swansea and particular interest, in describing to them

Scenes from Chaplin's "Gold Rush" (1925) which was
shown to packed audiences at the Picture House in 1927.
Authors collection

The outing to Cheddar Caves provided by Victor Cox for staff and workmen by charabancs in September 1921.
Courtesy of Clevedon Mercury

the various places visited was shown by their Clevedon colleagues who displayed considerable knowledge of the locality. Several of the old hands who had worked on the Picture House in earlier stages fell in with the party which also included Mr. Summerfield, representing Messrs. Gardiner Ltd., the Bristol engineering firm, Mr. Stokes, representing the Cardiff craftsmen who are completing the interior decoration of the building, and Mr. G.H. Eddy, the first tennant of the new shops at the Picture House. Many of the men brought their wives and children, not to mention the sweethearts, and, altogether it was quite a jolly gathering. The party arrived home safely about 11 pm all thoroughly pleased with the day's outing and fully appreciative of the skill and care of the charabanc drivers, especially in negotiating the difficult hills and turnings in the neighbourhood of Cheddar.

The outing was an appropriate finish-up to the many months of hard work entailed in completing the new Picture House which, as everyone can see for themselves, is a magnificent building and will add greatly to the enjoyment and comfort of Clevedon people, during the winter months, besides being a source of attraction for visitors, during the holiday season.

The opening which will take place quietly in a few days' time will reveal to its patrons the largest and most comfortable cinema in Somerset, with its artistic decorative scheme, its commodious balcony and its under-roof promenades. The proprietors are certainly to be congratulated on their enterprise which ought to benefit the town in many ways, besides enhancing its popularity.

The stage shows at the second Picture House mainly consisted of a pantomime at Christmas and at other times the stage was put to good use with Grand Concerts of which the first was early in 1929. A programme of the second concert staged on Sunday, 10 March 1929 is illustrated and the popularity of the concerts with patrons was such that they became a regular winter season event for a number of years.

Screen Lore

The Picture House was, as its name applies, a cinema and throughout the years many of the classics that cinema-goers came to cherish and have fond memories of found their way on to the screen and still do for no matter what the technology of today may provide for watching film be it via DVD, Video or on TV in the home there is still that special magic of seeing it in a place that is created for that purpose – in a cinema, an experience that cannot be created in any other way.

It would be difficult to list all of the films shown on the Clevedon cinemas screen since 1912 but lets pause for a while and look at a few pictures and some of the programmes. The Picture House, always screened a pre-dominance of British films. Way back in the early days of the cinema, in 1917 to be exact, from 24 to 27 November the film was 'The Life Of John Bunyan and 'Pilgrims Progress'. It was a two part film with 57 scenes. It was given the full treatment with a harmonium, something that was repeated on later occasions, and in the siege scenes depicted in John Bunyans life people were employed to make the necessary sound effects to accompany the scenes portrayed on the screen. The Harmonium was imported from the School opposite and situated below the screen providing the dramatic musical score along with a small Bijou orchestra. The film was described as a 'moving picture masterpiece' with the rider *The world's greatest Allegory brought to life before your eyes – Don't miss it*. It was shown three times daily at 3 pm, 7 pm and 8.30 pm.

Some other films which showed at the first Picture House between the years 1912 and 1920 give an idea of the product Victor Cox was providing for his patrons 'Wandering Jew', 'Guy Fawkes', 'Dick Turpins Ride To York', 'The Mysteries of Dr. Fu Man Chu', 'The Man With The Iron Foot' to mention a few. It is interesting to note that these were all British productions and I can find no records of films like 'Birth Of A Nation', 'Intolerance', epic productions by David Griffith and the like ever having been shown in the Picture House but then in those days renting imports was expensive and there being no real need to use expensive publicity to advertise films showing at the cinema, records are somewhat obscure.

Programmes produced at that time are interesting. Illustrated are the parts of one for November 1913. The main film is 'East Lynne' which was made in 1910. You will notice that the cast list is printed similar to a theatre programme as well the film content of five acts and 117 scenes and was 6,500 ft long. Mr Fitzpatrick's arms must have been aching after that one. Interesting too is the following three day programme which consists of one and two – reelers each having the footage noted. Just who made this film of 'East Lynne' is uncertain as a film was made of the novel by William Fox in 1916 which starred Theda Bara. It was re-made in 1925, again by William Fox, starring Alma Rubens. In the way in which it is described it would seem quite a home spun production as none of the cast are known but the film was another 'special' from Victor Cox for Clevedon picture-goers.

A month previous saw another 'special event' when 'Quo Vadis' was shown. Opening on 11 October 1913 for a full week, quite a rarity for the Picture House. For this screening the piano was augmented by strings and the phonograph. When the film of the book written by Henry Sienkiewicz in 1896 was actually made is obscure but it was almost certainly British and was the fore-runner of later films the best known being the MGM version in 1951 starring Robert Taylor, Deborah Kerr and Peter Ustinov.

In the programme for November 1929 the cinema is described as 'warm and cosy on the coldest day' and for a whole week (highly irregular) 'The King of Kings' (1927) was shown on the Picture House screen to full houses. The picture , made by Cecil B. de Mille and released by Pathe, was one of the last silent epics to be made. It starred H.B. Warner, an English actor who went to Hollywood in 1917, as Jesus. It is interesting to note that 'talkies' had been around for nearly two years before the Clevedon Picture House screened the silent epic. A full orchestra, an organ played by Victor Cox himself (it had recently been installed in the cinema) and the necessary sound effects were employed to support the film.

Using a full orchestra to augment the piano or Bijou musicians for important films was a special addition when prestige films were shown at the Picture House. Before the organ was installed

A programme for November 1929.
Authors collection

such accompaniment was achieved by borrowing the school harmonium from the school opposite as I have already mentioned and that was the case again when 'The Lost Chord' was screened, a picture I have no details of. When a few weeks later the film 'Ypres' was shown a big drum was used to echo the artillery. Sadly there is no record of who the musicians were who played at the Picture House but it is likely that they came from Clevedon or surrounding villages.

Saturday morning pictures started in 1920 even though Maximillian Corne seems to take the credit for it many years later. On 10 January was shown a performance of the film 'Sunnyside' (1919) which starred Charles Chaplin and Edna Purvience. It told the story of an overworked odd-job man who has a pastoral dream. It was a satirical film and seems a strange choice for children although of course there was the usual mixture of slapstick and chases.

The first time a cartoon film was shown took place on 3 June 1920. It was called 'Tramp, Tramp, Tramp' of which no details exist . Also shown on the same programme were local pictures of motor racing on the beach at Weston-super-Mare which were included in the 'newsreel' Gaumont Graphic. From then on a

The programme and scenes from Cecil B. Demille's "King of Kings" (1927) shown at the Picture House in November 1929. *Authors collection*

PROGRAMME

MONDAY, NOVEMBER 11th, FOR SIX DAYS

THE KING OF KINGS

A sincere, faithful and profoundly moving picture.

" I think it is a very beautiful picture, and everyone should go to see it," says the Bishop of London.

" Reverent, good and helpful." Bishop Bury.

PROGRAMME

MONDAY, NOVEMBER 18th, FOR THREE DAYS

SINS OF FASHION

Featuring ANDREE LAFAYETTE, SUZY PIERSON and MALCOLM TODD

Behind the scenes in a large fashion saloon. Also

THROUGH THE BREAKERS

Starring MARGARET LIVINGSTON and HOLMES HERBERT

A romance as glowing as the golden sands of its setting. From the play by Owen Davis.

COMEDY, INTEREST AND NEWS FILMS

cartoon was shown every Monday to Wednesday and a Gaumont Graphic newsreel every Thursday to Saturday.

In that year too, on 17 July 'Tarzan of the Apes' (1918) starring Elmo Lincoln was shown. It was the first of the Edgar Rice Borough's Tarzan films to be made. Showing more than two years after its release and by then the second Tarzan film had been made starring Gene Pollar in 'The Return of Tarzan' (1920) .

An interesting article appeared in the Picture House column of the *Clevedon Mercury* on the 6 March 1920.

Picture House, Clevedon

Monday next will bring the new serial, entitled 'The Red Glove'. The very latest thriller from the House of Serials, it should surpass in popularity anything yet put upon the market 'Brevity is the soul of wit' and this term might be applied to this picture. The producers have ' cut the cackle and come to the hosses' from the very beginning, and thrill follows thrill until each episode contains as much emotion as a long drama of five or six reels. The picture is full of marvellous stunts, which are not inserted in the end only but are perpetually cropping up in the unfolding of the story, which features that splendid horse-woman, Marie Walcamp. 'A Bit of Kindling' is the title of the long drama, (feature film) and Jackie Saunders, who is featured in this picture, will be found to give a splendid rendering of a most interesting part, about which the best advice we can offers, to see the film.

'Around The Town' is a really good feature in the programme, and to those who are familiar with the favourites of the moment in art, literature, and the science have a real treat in coming, as it were, face to face with their favourite writer or painter as the case may be. It is remarkable how very different these well known people are from what our imagination would have us believe them to be.

Thursday next 'Sweet Lavender' that well known play, will be shown and we have not the slightest doubt that it will be one of the episodes of the season, for there are few indeed who have not seen or at least heard of 'Sweet Lavender'. This film version has been so popular that it has been re-issued on two occasions. 'Elmo The Mighty' the serial of serials, is as full of go as ever and the comedy item will be 'Stateroom Secrets' followed by a very amusing interest 'Our Monkey Troubles' and the scene picture is 'Picturesque Australia'.

I make no apologies for transcribing that article in full as it describes a number of interests about the period. First the actual writing again is flowery and detailed, a style that was in vogue in those days. Did Victor Cox write that himself? The very full description of the film synopsis indicates an awareness of its content

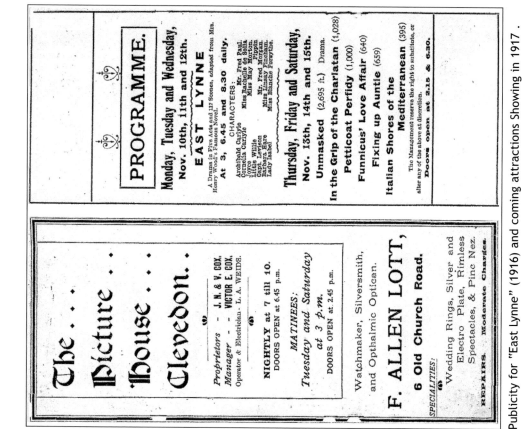

PROGRAMME.

Monday, Tuesday and Wednesday,
Nov. 10th, 11th and 12th.

EAST LYNNE

A Drama in Five Acts and 117 Scenes, adapted from Mrs.
Henry Wood's Famous Novel.

At 3, 6.45 and 8.30 daily.

CHARACTERS:

Archibald Carlyle — Mr. Fred Paul.
Cornelia Carlyle — Miss Rachelle de Solla
Joyce — Miss May Morton.
Little Willie — Miss May Pippin
Capt. Levison — Mr. Fred Morgan
Barbara Hare — Miss Lissey Finihan
Lady Isabel — Miss Blanche Forsythe.

Thursday, Friday and Saturday,
Nov. 13th, 14th and 15th.

Unmasked (2,695 ft.) Drama.

In the Grip of the Charlatan (1,028)

Petticoat Perfidy (1,000)

Funnicus' Love Affair (640)

Fixing up Auntie (659)

Italian Shores of the
Mediterranean (395)

The Management reserve the right to substitute, or
after any of the above at discretion.

Doors open at 2.15 & 6.30.

Tbe . . . .
Picture . . .
House . . . .
Clevedon . .

Proprietors — J. N. & V. COX.
Manager — VICTOR E. COX.
Operator & Electrician - L. A. WEEDS.

NIGHTLY at 7 till 10.
DOORS OPEN at 6.45 p.m.

MATINEES:
Tuesday and Saturday
at 3 p.m.
DOORS OPEN at 2.45 p.m.

Watchmaker, Silversmith,
and Opthalmic Optican.

F. ALLEN LOTT,
6 Old Church Road.

SPECIALITIES:

Wedding Rings, Silver and
Electro Plate, Rimless
Spectacles, & Pince Nez.

REPAIRS. Moderate Charges.

Publicity for "East Lynne" (1916) and coming attractions Showing in 1917 .

Both Authors collection

PICTURE HOUSE

Old Church Road, CLEVEDON.

Monday, Tuesday & Wednesday, Nov. 24th, 25th & 26th

At 3, 7, & 8.30 Daily. AT USUAL PRICES.

One Shilling Seats (Numbered and Reserved) can be booked every evening
from 7 till 10, and on Tuesdays and Saturdays from 3 till 6.30.

THE LIFE OF
JOHN BUNYAN

AND "PILGRIM'S PROGRESS."

A Moving Picture Masterpiece.

Publicity for the weeks following the opening of the
first Picture House in 1912.

92

though such information was often released by the distributors. More interestingly again the mix of programming features with the supporting subjects covering comedy, interest and the ever popular serial. Serials were shown every performance with eventually two different ones each week, a change being made on Thursday. One starring the serial queen we all have heard about, Pearl White, was 'The Lightening Raider' (1916) in fifteen episodes was screened at the Picture House some five years after its making.

A sample of the publicity for films showing at the cinema provided by the distributor is illustrated using a postcard with details of a serial showing at the Picture House in 1917. The card obtained from the cinema for a penny or so could be sent to friends etc. (see page 27)

In closing the silent era of the cinema it is interesting to note in the period March 1920 to May 1923 there were a total of 230 feature films shown by the two Picture Houses. Of these 127 were British and the remaining mostly from Hollywood. It is also noted that popular stars from the movie capital had very little exposure at the cinema. For instance there were only four features starring Charles Chaplin, Dustin Farnum 5, Douglas Fairbanks Snr 1, Mary Pickford 1 and Nazimova 3 and there were two Tarzan films. (Features were films of more than four reels.)

One film worth a mention is 'Flag Lieutenant' which was a film about the Boxer uprising in China. When it was shown at the Picture House a fourteen piece orchestra was squeezed into the small orchestra pit giving forth spiritedly 'Pomp and Circumstance' at every opportune moment supported by the Harmonium and Blanche rendering appropriate arias to suit. It was recorded as being the most spectacular show of the cinema's silent era. Three films were made of 'Flag Lieutenant'. The first was in 1919 which starred George Wynn. A remake in 1926 starred Henry Edwards who was a popular British star of the silent screen. Born in Weston-super-Mare in 1883 not only was he an actor but also a director, writer and producer. He starred again in the leading role in the talkie remake in 1933. The 1926 version would have been the one shown and being the resounding success at the Picture House with overflowing houses every performance.

When talkies came to the cinema in 1930 all of that changed of course. The first feature film shown in the Picture House I have already described elsewhere in the book but still Victor Cox clung heavily towards British pictures. Many of the well known and remembered 'talkies' of the 1930s do not seem to have appeared at the Clevedon house though many of the British comedies of the day did with regular appearances of George Formby, Old Mother Riley, Jack and Claude Hulbert, Will Hay and many others who regularly found themselves on the Picture House screen albeit two or three years late.

The Curzon Cinema

www.curzon.org.uk
Old Church Road, Clevedon, BS21 6NN
Tel 01275 87 1000

DEC 2003/FEB 2004

FRI 12th DEC for 7 Nights at 7.45
plus MON 15th at 2.00pm
LOVE ACTUALLY (15)
(US 2003) dir: Richard Curtis 2hr 15min
Colin Firth, Emma Thompson, Hugh Grant, Martine McCutcheon, Bill Nighy, Laura Linney, Alan Rickman

This ensemble comedy tells ten separate but intertwining stories of love in London, leading up to a big climax on Christmas Eve.

SUN 14th at 5.00pm (D/O 4.45pm) **and Tue 16th DEC at 2.00pm**
MEET ME IN ST LOUIS (U) NEW PRINT
(US 1944) dir: Vincente Minnelli 1hr 50mins
Judy Garland, Margaret O'Brien, Mary Astor, Lucille Bremer

Vintage MGM musical, with dazzling musical numbers such as 'Have Yourself a Merry Little Christmas and Skip to My Lou. It provides a romanticised but still uplifting depiction of life in turn-of-the-century St Louis, with Mary Astor as mom and Judy Garland as one of her four daughters, this is a tale that only works against the backdrop of a more innocent age. "Too good to miss" *Radio Times*

FRI 19th DEC for TWO WEEKS
Fri 19th to Tues 23rd at 7.45pm AND Sat 27th to Tues 30th at 7.45pm
plus
Sat 20th to Weds 24th at 2.00pm, Sat 27th to Wed 31st at 2.00pm AND Fri 2nd Jan to Sun 4th Jan at 2.00pm
FINDING NEMO (U) 7.45
(US 2003) dir: Andrew Stanton 1hr 44min
voices of: Albert Brooks, Ellen DeGeneres, John Ratzenberger
Animated adventure following the eventful journey of clownfish Marlin and his son Nemo. After being separated from his father Nemo finds himself captured and in a dentist's fish tank in Sydney, Australia. Marlin forming a friendship with a fish called Dory sets out on the dangerous quest to find Nemo and return home.

We will be closed in the evening on Christmas Eve, all day Christmas Day and Boxing Day. Also, we are closed in the evening on New Year's Eve and all day New Year's Day. We wish you all a very Merry Christmas and a happy and prosperous New Year.

FRI 2nd JAN for 7 Nights at 7.45
MASTER & COMMANDER (12A)
(UK 2003) dir: Peter Weir 2hr 15min
Russell Crowe, Paul Bettany, James D'Arcy, Edward Woodall

Set during the Napoleonic Wars in 1806, this is the seafaring adventuring tale of the British ship, HMS Surprise, captained by 'Lucky' Jack Aubrey (Crowe) who travels around the world with his friend and secret agent, Stephen Maturin, in an era where the open seas were the vast and wild setting for amazing adventures and high intrigue.

Tue 6th & Thur 8th JAN at 2.00pm
MASTER & COMMANDER (12A)
(UK 2003) dir: Peter Weir 2hr 15min
Russell Crowe, Paul Bettany, James D'Arcy, Edward Woodall

FRI 9th JAN for 6 Nights (NOT Sun 11th) **at 7.45**
plus SUN 11th at 5.00pm
FREAKY FRIDAY (PG)
(US 2003) dir: Mark Waters 1hr 36min
Jamie Lee Curtis, Harold Gould, Lindsay Lohan, Mark Harmon

Dr. Tess Coleman and her fifteen-year-old daughter, Anna don't see eye-to-eye on clothes, hair, music, and certainly not in each other's taste in men. One Thursday evening, their disagreements reach a fever pitch - Anna is incensed that her mother doesn't support her musical aspirations and Tess, a widow about to remarry, can't see why Anna won't give her fiance a break. Everything soon changes when two identical Chinese fortune cookies cause a little mystic mayhem. The next morning, their Friday gets freaky when Tess and Anna find themselves inside the wrong bodies.

SUN 11th DEC for 1 Night - FILM CLUB
(Temporary Membership (£1) available on the door) DOORS OPEN 8.15pm
Etre et Avoir 8.30 Cert U
(Fr 2002) dir: Nicolas Philibert 1hr 44min
Documentary, Subtitled

"This wonderful film charts half a year in the life of Georges Lopez and the infant & junior pupils he teaches at a tiny single class school in Auvergne. A witty, hugely moving study of dedication, intelligence and downright goodness, this small gem covers all this and more, it's one of the very finest films you're likely to see in a long time. Just beautiful" TIME OUT

Tue 13th JAN at 2.00pm
Etre et Avoir (U)
(Fr 2002) dir: Nicolas Philibert 1hr 44m
Documentary, Subtitled

Thur 15th JAN at 2.00pm
FREAKY FRIDAY (PG)
(US 2003) dir: Mark Waters 1hr 36min
Jamie Lee Curtis, Harold Gould, Lindsay Lohan, Mark Harmon

FRI 16th JAN for 3 Nights
IN THE CUT (18)
(US/Australia 2003) dir: Jane Campion 1hr 59mins
Meg Ryan, Mark Ruffalo, Jennifer Jason Leigh, Kevin Bacon

Frannie Thorstin (Ryan) is an English teacher at New York University, caught up in a murder case when a 'disarticulated' corpse shows up on her doorstep. Frannie had seen the girl having sex the day before with a guy bearing an uncanny resemblance to the homicide detective now investigating her death, Gio Molloy (Ruffalo).

MON 19th JAN for 4 Nights at 7.45
CALENDAR GIRLS (12A)
(US 2003) dir: Nigel Cole 1hr 48mins
Helen Mirren, Julie Walters

Tricia (Mirren) and Angela (Walters) are members of the WI - who suggested the group pose naked -- with strategically placed objects protecting their modesty -- to raise money for leukaemia research after Angela's husband John died from the disease.

Tue 20th & Thur 22nd JAN at 2.00pm
MANSFIELD PARK (15)
(UK 1999) dir: Patricia Rozema 1hr 52m
Jonny Lee Miller, Frances O'Connor, Embeth Davidtz, Lindsay Duncan

Jane Austen's third novel of principled innocents courted by shallow sophisticates, complete with sex, drugs and contemporary cynicism. "Delectably performed, and beautifully measured by Rozema, whose light, fluid touch conveys the story along on a nod and a wink." TIME OUT

FRI 23rd JAN for 7 Days
COLD MOUNTAIN (15) 7.45 INTERMISSION
(US 2003) dir: Anthony Minghella 2hr 30mins
Brendan Gleeson, Jude Law, Nicole Kidman, Renée Zellweger

The Civil War reaches its final days, Inman a wounded soldier, gets up out of what doctors thought was his death bed, and begins the walk to his home in North Carolina on Cold Mountain. Waiting there for him is the woman he left behind.

Tue 27th & Thur 29th JAN at 2.00pm
COLD MOUNTAIN (15) INTERMISSION
(US 2003) dir: Anthony Minghella 2hr 30mins
Brendan Gleeson, Jude Law, Nicole Kidman, Renée Zellweger

FRI 30th JAN for 6 Nights (NOT Sun 1st at 7.00)
plus SUN 1st FEB at 2.00pm
LORD OF THE RINGS: (12A)
The Return of the King
(NZ 2003) dir: Peter Jackson 3hr 21mins INTERMISSION
Cate Blanchett, Elijah Wood, Sean Astin, Sir Ian McKellen

The third of the trilogy. As the shadow of Mordor grows across the land, Aragorn is revealed as the hidden heir to the ancient kings. Gandalf miraculously returns and defeats the evil wizard, Saruman. Sam leaves his master for the dead after a battle with the giant spider, Shelob; but Frodo is still alive—in the hands of the Orcs. And while the armies of the Dark Lord are massing—and the one ring comes ever closer to the Cracks of Doom.

SUN 1st FEB for 1 Night - FILM CLUB
(Temporary Membership (£1) available on the door) DOORS OPEN 8.15pm
THE MOTHER 8.30 Cert: 15
(UK 2003) dir: Roger Michell 1hr 51m
Anne Reid, Daniel Craig

"Scripted by Hanif Kureishi, Anne Reid is the recently widowed May, who comes down to stay with her middle-class son in London and can't find the courage to leave. Even then it's only her son's friend Darren (Craig) who sees May as a person, not an antiquated nuisance. They become friends, then, secretly, lovers. Reid is wonderful, subtly revealing a difficult, long-time repressed woman coming out of her shell under the attentive curiosity of the younger man." *Time Out*

Tue 3rd & Thur 5th FEB at 2.00pm
LORD OF THE RINGS: (12A)
The Return of the King
(NZ 2003) dir: Peter Jackson 3hr 21mins INTERMISSION
Sir Ian McKellen, Elijah Wood, Sean Astin, Cate Blanchett, Liv Tyler, Viggo Mortensen, Karl Urban, Miranda Otto

INFORMATION

Visit our website: www.curzon.org.uk
Or by WAP: tagtag.com/curzon

Tickets: Adults: **£4.00**
Concs: **£3.00** (Until 15s £4.00 & £4.80)
(Ticket Prices will go up on 2nd January 2004 to £4.50 & £3.50)

Doors Open: 30mins before film start times.

No Smoking: We are a no smoking cinema.

Parking: Free car-parking in Great Western Rd. (50mtrs)

Disabled Access: The CURZON currently has limited access for disabled people, we provide separate wheelchair and an ambulant access. We have toilet facilities (RADAR key) and an infra-red hearing loop/headsets. Please ask for details.

Charitable Donations: As a registered charity the CURZON needs your support to keep operating. Please complete the form (available from the foyer) to make a gift aid donation towards its restoration and continued operation.

Gift Vouchers: Why not give CURZON gift vouchers - £4.50 & £3.50 - the ideal present.

Mailing List: The CURZON programme can be sent to you by post. Complete the slip overleaf and return it with a cheque or postal order for £3.00 for one year's mailing.

The Curzon Community cinema programme for the period December 2004 to February 2004.

During the 1940s, half of which was dogged with conflict, more Hollywood product was shown at the cinema than in its entire previous life. Films such as 'Gone With The Wind' (1939), 'Wizard of Oz'(1939), 'Casablanca' (1942) and many other epics found their way on to the screen though very late indeed. There was still a predominance of British films with possibly every one made getting a showing or repeat showing with the Ealing comedies to the fore stretching well into the 50s.

In 1956 the Maxime, as it was then, went over to Cinemascope and as mentioned earlier the first film in that format shown was, yes a British production, 'Cockleshell Heroes'. Times were changing though as fewer British films were available and the major titles from 'tinsel town' began to appear on the Clevedon screen. During the 1980s there was near total dependence on Hollywood with blockbusters like the 'Star Wars' trilogy, 'The Omen' 'The Entity' and many others catering now for a different audience though family audiences were finding films from Walt Disney regularly on screen. One blessing with all of this was that films were reaching the Curzon only a short time after release thanks to an enlightened booking system.

The Curzon had an incursion into late night showing in 1972 when on Thursday 24th there was a midnight matinee with the showing of 'Frankenstein Created Woman' (1968) starring our old friend Peter Cushing and 'Plague of the Zombies' (1965) with Andre Morell. Rather than a foray into late night showing as a policy I feel that this one show, for there were no others advertised, was perhaps some sort of Charity or publicity event.

Today the latest films are now shown only a week or two after national release but there is still that tradition of showing films British whenever they are available.

12. The Oak Room

The last part of the second Picture House to be fitted out was the Oak Room Café. It is though that originally offices were envisaged for the first floor and that a restaurant was an afterthought. The Oak Room was a splendid affair with a lounge area and polished floor. It was decorated with elegant furnishings of the period, a commodious settee and accommodated a grand piano. The semi-circular stained glass window filled one wall. Through double doors one passed in to the restaurant running the length of the upper floor ending with the service area and the kitchen. It was designed and furnished with oak panelling and offered twenty-five covers. The windows fronting Old Church Road also had stained glass. It opened on Monday, 12 June 1922 and was an immediate success.

The main entrance to the restaurant led up from Old Church Road through one of the shop units which today is a florists. The two tiers of stairs led into the Oak Room itself. This was most certainly the general access and exit from the restaurant and the post of the balustrade can just be seen lower off-centre of the picture of the interior.

The restaurant served morning coffee, lunches, afternoon teas and after show dinners and was well appointed with a silver service. At once the Oak Room became a popular venue for wedding receptions almost up to its eventual closure. Some cinema staff held their receptions there. So popular was it, I am told, that on one Saturday alone three such receptions were held in the cinema's restaurant.

In the beginning, the Oak Room was managed by Mrs Blanche Cox. Mrs Edwards, of Parnell Road, remembers her well as she worked under her as a cook presumably towards the end of or shortly after the second world war. She describes Blanche Cox as being a short lady who set her hair curls using a skewer heated in the gas fire. She ran a very tight regime and expected everything to be just so especially the laying-up so much so that she was in demand for that service at the local American war bases when they had important visitors to entertain. At this time the waitresses in the Oak Room wore dresses made from the redundant blackout material. They were shiny and complete with tiny aprons which matched the table clothes. Mrs Edwards also remembers that if any black soldiers were to visit the cinema they were not allowed to eat in the Oak Room and had to manage in the Lounge area away from the main seated area (presumably on the orders of their Military).

The Oak Room suffered great damage when the bomb exploded opposite the entrance to the cinema in January 1941. All of the stained glassed windows were blown out and the mess in the Oak Room itself was devastating. The worst hit was the semi-circular window in the Lounge area which was completely destroyed. (This is described in Chapter 8.) It was eventually sealed off as can be seen by close inspection of the stonework over the present cinema entrance.

During the Second World War, there was a war-work factory next to the cinema and the Oak Room was used as a workers canteen where at least one 'Workers Playtime' was recorded for later broadcasting on the BBC Light programme. Unfortunately there are no actual details available but some favourite wartime stars appeared regularly in this very popular morale-boosting radio show.

Alas the restaurant fell on less favourable times and after many years of service to the people of Clevedon it closed. Exactly when that was is obscure but an advertisement from the 1950s still informs that the Oak Room Café at the Maxime Cinema is open for morning coffee 10 am to Noon, for Luncheons 12.30 to 2 pm and Teas 3 pm to 6.30 pm At that time it was run by T. Wilkinson who also seemingly had concessions at the Salthouse Buffet (Salthouse Fields), Pier Snack Bar and the Pavilion during all concerts and dances. There are however no such announcements after the cinema became the Curzon and one must assume that the Oak Room closed as a café around that time.

Since its demise it has been a shoe shop, Gallery, book store and finally a storage room. The kitchen area was used at one time by Clevedon Fisheries for preparing fresh fish for sale in the shop below.

All credit then to the present Managers who have ensured the Oak Room has been partially restored to its former condition the oak panelling cleaned and returned to what is probably its best condition for fifty years or so and is now available again for Community use. It is intended that eventually it will be returned to a full restaurant and a tradition was revived when in 2003 the room was used once more for a wedding reception being that of Mr D. and Mrs F. Moores.

The Oak Room Café
in the 1920s.
*Courtesy of Clevedon
Mercury*

An advertisement for the
Oak Room Café during the
days of the Maxime cinema.
Authors collection

Oak Room Cafe

AND   C.H.A.

CAKE SHOP

Maxime Cinema, Old Church Road, CLEVEDON

MORNING COFFEE, 10 to 12 noon   LUNCHEONS, 12.30 to 2 p.m.
TEAS, 3 to 6.30 p.m.

SALTHOUSE BUFFET (Salthouse Fields), and
PIER SNACK BAR .... Tea, Refreshments, Ices
THE PAVILION ...... Refreshments during all
Concerts and Dances

WE SPECIALISE IN ALL FORMS OF CATERING

Sole Proprietor : T. WILKINSON, Oak Room Cafe

Telephone 2612

Renovated Oak Room
panelling undertaken
by volunteers in
2003.
Authors collection

The Oak Room after renovation in 2003. The setting is for the first wedding reception for over fifty years in the room therefore restoring a traditional use for which the Oak Room was well-known locally. It is recorded that on one Saturday alone three receptions were held in the room whilst the normal film programme was going on in the cinema.
Courtesy of County Gardens Florists, Clevedon

13. Clevedon In the Movies

Thus far this book about the motion-picture in Clevedon has dealt mostly with its cinema which of course it has been, and still is, the major venue for such activity in the town. That is not to say no other venue has been used for the exhibition of motion-pictures in the town. Throughout the years there must have been charity and private shows attended by many of people in Public and Church halls in the town and district and one can go right back to the early days of Victor Cox and probably others who had the equipment to show the primitive fledgling phenomenon.

As will be noted in the section on Portishead there was a Mr Donne who ran cinema there in the late 20s. He also ran films in Nailsea and Clevedon though little is known about these. The actual location in Clevedon is also unknown but likely the shows were run in the Public Hall and in direct competition with the Picture House. For how long these shows continued is also obscure but because of developments in Portishead it was unlikely to have been beyond 1932. These shows would have been of little concern to Cox I would think.

Throughout the land many towns and cities can lay claim to having 'been in the movies' and Clevedon is no exception. Way back in 1903 Victor Cox commissioned a professional film company (the name unfortunately not recorded) to make an 'animatograph' advertising the town as it was in those days. The title was 'Clevedon – As Others See Us' and was apparently well received. A copy of the film, it may be the original, still exists but because of the highly volatile condition, it being nitrate film stock which is flammable, that copy is now held in vaults at the British Film Institute. Fortunately a 16 mm copy was made of it many years ago which is held in the Curzon Film Archive.

The film records scenes depicting the very early years of the 20th Century with children going to school, people on the beach and views of the sea front. Included also are shots of Captain Rowles (Piermaster?), Mr Simms and Mr Rogers, gentlemen who must have had some importance in Clevedon of that time. Perhaps someone will be able to enlighten. At some stage however, in the 16 mm copy, we move up to the First World War with 1915 shots of troops marching through Clevedon. A large contingent of the Lancashire Regiment, some 2000 troops, arrived in Clevedon on 23 June of that year. They were billeted in every available space in and around the town. The scenes suggest the film was made of their march through the town soon after their arrival. There are also scenes of training for trench warfare.

'Clevedon As Others See Us (1903) was shown at the Picture House week commencing 14 October 1912.

Legend has it that Victor Cox, in an interview with a BBC presenter in July 1961, thought that the original 1903 film had been lost. He had told Stan Newton to get rid of it many years before because being nitrate stock it was dangerous and illegal to keep in a cinema projection room. Stan did not get rid of it however, and it landed up in the hands of a Mr Caple who lived in St. Andrews Drive. What happened to it then is not known but in 1997 it found its way back to where it had started, at the cinema. Unable to keep the 35 mm film because of the regulations and unable to show it on modern projectors the British Film Institute agreed to take it into their vaults.

There are other films too in the Archive recording life in Clevedon. The pier and the fight to save it, technology changes at Clevedon's own newspaper *The Mercury* and other reels of local interest are preserved. The Curzon itself has featured on a number of professionally produced videos which have received nation-wide broadcast. Clevedon has of course also been featured in a number of cinema and television productions which also have received world-wide distribution.

Perhaps the film which captures the spirit of the town best is Clevedon's own film 'Festival 70'. The film records a week of colour, fun and entertainment which took place between 13 and 21 June 1970. At the period of time in which the M5 motorway was being constructed and it exemplifies the community spirit which went into one week in the life of the town. All of these films are now preserved in the Film Archive of the Curzon cinema.

14. The Everlasting Picture Show

Motion-pictures have endured for a hundred years or thereabouts in Clevedon and its environs and in the two cinema buildings continuously for well over ninety years. Not only is this a phenomenon but also unique, certainly in this country. It can claim proudly to be an Everlasting Picture Show.

Somehow the trials and tribulations of the motion-picture industry have by-passed the cinema in Clevedon. It is as if its existence has been completely overlooked. Of course there are cinemas whose buildings are as old as the present Clevedon cinema and yes some of those are once again on films. I say again because sometime in their history they have either closed and then re-opened or have been on Bingo or other similar entertainment. There are those that have undergone changes into furniture warehouses, garages, pubs and restaurant businesses and sadly those that have been demolished and have gone forever the sites now supermarkets, car parks and worse.

The modest little cinema built in 1912 and its successor which eventually enveloped it have kept pictures going for 92 years at the time of writing. Changed, modified, altered and even bombed the old rebuilt Picture House is still with us. Why has Clevedon's cinema lasted when so many others have become lost forever?

To be sure at the time of its building the Picture House was described as one of the most luxurious and grand in the West. It was, however, little different to other provincial cinemas built around that time though it has to be said some were excellent, the Whiteladies at Bristol to name just one. Credit due to Victor Cox but he was no cinema architect. The well known cinema builders of the day such as Frank Wilkins, William Henry Watkins, Cecil Massey or even 'local' builders of the cinemas in nearby Bristol did not figure in Cox's plans. It would have been too costly. Possibly this is why the cinema has suffered from obscurity throughout its long life. When taken over in 1996 it was discovered that very little was known nationally of the present Curzon or its uniqueness. Sparse insertions in the Kinematograph Year books and articles in the local paper are all that can be found about the cinema's history in the world at large.

Since 1996 this is being remedied with recognition by national bodies such as the Cinema Theatre Association. Whilst it has little architectural merit it remains an example of a 1920s cinema few of which remain in the country today and still on film to boot. It is simply unique and for those of us who have custodian-ship and work within it the pleasure is immense but will that be enough to, at least, reach the Centenary in 2012 and beyond?

What of the future? It would be presumptuous, even foolish, to make any predictions here. The cinema business for independents is fraught with problems of keeping going and being able to pay the bills alongside the need to be an alternative to the nearest multiplex with its diversity of programming and ability to provide what its customers seek from a visit to the pictures. By and large, regardless of what we may feel about the multiplexes they do a very good job and they certainly have done much to reinstate cinema as the prime and preferred movie entertainment experience once more.

The Curzon has four multiplex operations and a Film Centre on its doorstep not to mention two city centre cinemas, a suburban cinema plus art houses in Bristol. Its scoring point is in its locality for the local community is not forced to travel very far for their cinema entertainment should they not wish to and its homely 'next door' atmosphere.

The Curzon is limited not only by what product it can show but when it can show it. Probably unknown to the reader the film distributors have an important say in what a cinema can show if it is a mainstream house with only one screen. If a film is to be booked for a national release date showing the cost is very high to the cinema so films tend to reach the Curzon three weeks or even more after release Nationally. Add to that the number of copies of the film available at any given time can also have serious consequences for the Curzon if there is a shortage of copies. This can happen when a film is a 'sleeper' and unexpectedly becomes popular in the multiplexes and their copies are retained for extra weeks. None of this helps cinemas such as the Curzon because they may not be able to maintain good occupancy (audience) figures if everyone has decided they cannot wait and gone elsewhere to see the film. That remedy is obvious.

The Curzon suffers from years of neglect, do-it-yourself or not at all and 'we can't afford it' brand of mentality. Thankfully this changed in November 1996. For many of those involved in the saving of the cinema not too much was known about running a cinema especially when it was a seven day mainstream operation like the Curzon but the lacking in skills and knowledge was countered by a willingness and determination to save Britain's oldest working cinema site.

Much has been achieved since that Autumn evening in November 1996 when, again without a break in performances holding up the tradition, the Curzon had new owners. With a small paid staff and a goodly number of volunteers it has not only kept going but improved with the up-dating of first its technical equipment and now the seating, services, a small cosmetic refurbishment and more importantly ownership.

In those heady days of 1996 plans were put forward to 'return the cinema to its former glory' and it is here that I have many reservations about the bold and perhaps exciting plans then put before the public. Quite what 'former glory' really means brings many questions to mind. It was built as a silent cinema complete with its unique panelling which may have passed in the talkie days of 50 years ago but modern cinema sound today demands totally different acoustics. Removal of the false ceiling is bound to aggravate the present problems. No doubt this can be overcome but at what cost? Just what will the picture look like from the rear of the Balcony compared with today's wall to wall screens found in many cinemas.

In the grandiose scheme of things the cinema will become a Centre for the arts. Good and noble sentiments and aims but will it work in years to come and will the importance of it being a cinema be diminished. Do we really need photographic rooms and the like with digital photography now affordable and relegating traditional photography to a minority following. Recording studios will be expensive though an excellent facility for the local radio station and educational purposes but, will the local radio station be able to function as it does at present, that also being a community enterprise and is quite expensive to run and has demand upon community support. Access to computer and Information Technology is already well catered for.

There has been for sometime opposition to the design of the new entrance though personally I have no axe to grind here providing it is tasteful. I only mention these points to illustrate that at the time of writing this book there are many and varied problems ahead – and that is without delving into the vast amount of money that has to be found to carry out these ambition plans and operate them. How will that be achieved? It will be a monumental task which perhaps the local populace will not be able to sustain. Only time and continued support, particularly with 'bums on seats', will tell.

These matters however are not the concern of this book. It is about motion-pictures in Clevedon and district. I have not written it as just another historical book or a reminiscence of the past but as a **celebration** of what is nearly one hundred years of motion-pictures exhibition in Clevedon and how it has been achieved and has become

The Everlasting Picture Show

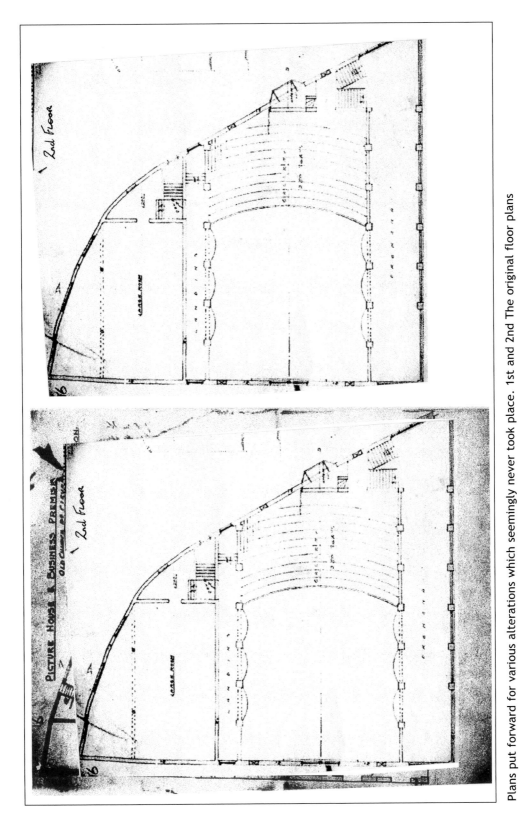

Plans put forward for various alterations which seemingly never took place. 1st and 2nd The original floor plans

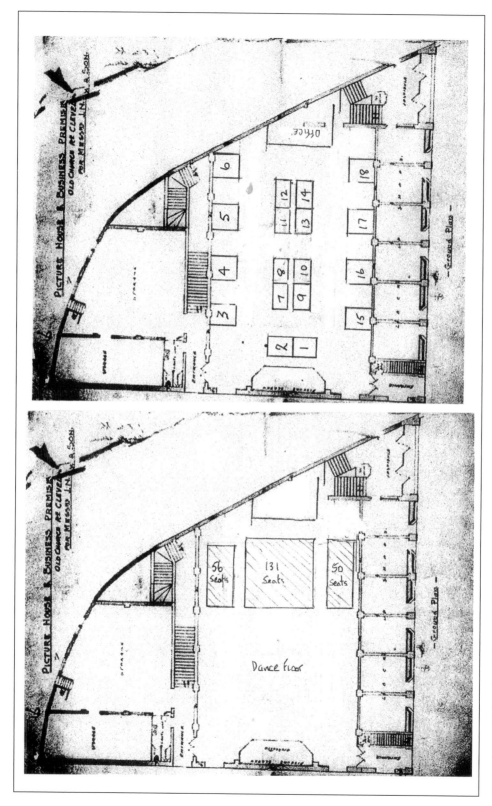

More plans which gained obscurity. 3rd. plan is for converting the stalls into a dance floor. 4th. plan suggests complete conversion of the stalls area into a Market Hall.

PORTISHEAD

CINEMA

Authors Note

Finding authentic information about the cinema at Portishead has not been an easy task for there appears to be very little written about its existence and the fact that it closed so many years ago and before the time of many present residents. I am indebted to Kenneth Crowhurst for his help and the fact that he alone seems to have been responsible for writing down much from which research for this story was made possible. I am also grateful for the assistance received from Alfred Poole, Jim and Mary Dyer and to Gina Scarbro without whose help this account of the cinema's existence could not have been written.

If there are errors and omissions please accept that every effort has been made to verify that which is written here and please accept my apologies should any come to light.

Maurice Thornton

1. Introduction

Portishead, a little to the North of Clevedon and on the estuary of the River Avon has a history going back to Roman times and possibly before. It has always been associated, as its position dictates, with the sea and as a port from which it gets its name 'a port at the head of the river'. The town is built on a small tributary and its main architecture is Victorian. In the early part of the 19th century a deep water dock was built to service the larger ships that brought commerce from across the world and to export materials such as coal. Well known and visible for miles was the power station with its four chimney stacks which for many years were a welcoming sign for anyone living locally as they travelled home crossing the motorway bridge over the River Avon. Alas they are no more.

A pleasant town with its busy main thoroughfare has seen much change through the years and never more so than at the turn of the century with its Marina development and large housing schemes. There is little to remind one of its past the sea trade, nail factory and power station now history and the seaward spaces dominated by warehousing and concrete.

There is one small reminder of the past that still exists however. Nestling between stone built properties at the end of the High Street quite near to where the original sea port and docks were sited stands the present Library. This building has seen three changes in its life of over a century-and-a-half, first as a meeting hall, then a cinema and finally, to date, as the local library. This is the story of the early life of the building and Portishead's little cinema.

The Portishead Cinema. This picture was probably taken in early 1950's. It shows the entrance with the overhead cinema sign and a display board propped against the entrance. *Courtesy of Kenneth Crowhurst*

2. The Assembly Hall

As far as I can discover in the mid 19th Century there was need to provide a suitable place for the social entertainment of residents of the bustling village of Portishead which by 1848 was thriving and developing rapidly. The docks had not yet been built and the Pyll (Pill) still ran right up to the High Street. Around the middle of the century a small hall was built just off the High Street, part of which is still in evidence today. It was built by Public subscription and by public need and was established as the Assembly Hall. It was not designed to be architecturally significant but adequate at the time for meetings and small gatherings and the predominant social and cultural needs of the day.

The advent of moving pictures was as yet many years in the future and the only projected picture presentation at that time was by slide lantern, usually given by well-known lanternists. The mid-nineteenth-century Victorians loved 'magic lantern' shows and one can be sure of occasional highly entertaining performances given in the Assembly Hall.

Research suggests that the Hall became to small to cater for the increasing social needs of the village. Portishead was rapidly becoming a town and having received a branch railway line from the Bristol & Exeter main line it was reaping the benefits with an influx of residents and trade that the railways brought.

A new Assembly Hall was opened on the 5 January 1893. The old hall had been extensively altered adding seating for around 200 people. There had been constructed a lofty lantern roof allowing a considerable improvement of natural light into the hall. To open the new hall a concert was organised by the organist of the Parish Church, Mr W.T. Roe which was described as an outstanding success. During the following weeks more such concerts were organised to which, according to the Clevedon Mercury, the votaries of Terpischore 'express delight with the Hall and the accommodation it affords'.

Internally, after the alterations, the Hall had one large main area with a stage at one end and entrance foyer which was reached from street level first by steps and later by a ramp. Double doors led into the main hall which was quite lofty and well lit in the daytime by the lantern roof which also afforded some ventilation. Each side of the stage were two further rooms which shared the use as meeting rooms and dressing rooms for stage shows etc. The interior décor rose to no more than dark wood and cream coloured walls lighting being by gas but by 1916 electric lighting had been installed. There was no orchestra pit but a piano was positioned down front of the stage.

The new Assembly Hall it seems did not last very long. It is recorded that on the 15 November 1893 the New Assembly Hall re-opened. This rather suggests that it had closed at some time prior to that date for further alteration. There had apparently been some concerns about the ventilation, egress and lavatories expressed by the local Magistrates when considering the application to license the Assembly Hall for theatrical performances. This time the seating had been increased to 350 persons, new lavatories, improved ventilation and new exits were all provided as well as cloakrooms. These changes to plans allowed for the enlargement of the Hall to take place.

The first notation that the Assembly Hall had been used for a Cinematograph performance comes in 1906. The programme is not known and it is likely that it was either given by a local resident who owned a projector or possibly a visiting speaker, or even a travelling Bioscope show. Considering the purpose of the Assembly Hall there would certainly have been 'living picture' show presentations from time to time.

Motion-picture presentation in the Assembly Hall must have taken place quite regularly prior to the First World War but the first mention of a 'Portishead cinema' comes for 9 November 1915 when there were special programmes in aid of the Cinematograph trade appeal to raise £30,000 nationally to provide a convoy of motor ambulances and other vehicles to help bring home the thousands of wounded troops from France. There were two shows at 6.30 pm and 8.30 pm and the films were supplied by Pathe Freres Ltd. of London and the Bristol Film Service. The Assembly Hall was given over free of charge by MrS.Thomas who presumably was the manager or perhaps head of a group administering the Hall.

The High Street, Portishead. The posters on the wall by the shop are believed to be advertising a Cinematograph show in the Assembly Hall and it is thought it was probably the first public commercial show of 'living pictures' in the village.
(Unknown)

The Assembly Hall was crowded to overflowing for the two shows. Among the films shown were scenes of wounded soldiers from the Dardanells campaign, a three-part comedy and a four-part American Civil War drama 'The Grey Sentinel' (1913). There were many helpers selling tickets and the prize for selling the most was won by Miss Ida Orchard. It is not recorded however how much was raised for the Cinema Ambulance Fund.

By this time cinematograph shows were quite regular and in fact reference to a 'Portishead Cinema Management' gives the impression that they were an important part of the entertainment available at the Assembly Hall. A programme for 25 and 27 November 1915 describes the Management has having secured the fine historical drama 'When Rome Ruled'. (1913). A picture in five parts it blended the scenes together with a narrative telling the story of life in the days of Julius Caesar and the persecution of the Christians. It had no 'stars' nevertheless it thrilled the Portishead audiences.

By 1916 the cinema was running Thursday and Saturday each week. Prices of admission were 4d., 5d. and 7d. Children were admitted to a matinee only (thought to be Saturday afternoon) for 2d. and 3d. Good programmes had been secured. For the 'week' of 15 January a special long programme was secured which included two fine dramas 'The Potters Wheel' and 'The Gamblers' which were two two-part comedies.

The following 'week' saw what was described as the 'longest show ever to be shown in Portishead' at that time with 'King of the Forest' (1914) and a military drama 'Two Lads and a Lassie' (1914) plus comedies and a serial making nine different pictures in all. It must be remembered though that each film would have lasted no more than twenty minutes.

There were promises of further elation with Keystone comedies and Chaplin films to come in future weeks and to delight the patrons the magnificent production of 'The Sign of the Cross' (1915) starring William Farnum.

For the 'week' of 31 August and 2 September 1916 the film 'Vanity Fair' was advertised. It is not known which version this was. A film was made of the famous Thackery novel in 1911 by Vitagraph which starred Helen Gardner as Becky Sharp who by 1913 had fallen by the wayside in pictures. Another version was made in 1915 by Edison which starred Minnie Fiske (billed as Mrs Fiske) as Becky. This was to be her last silent film also as she returned to the stage following completion. I would say that it was the second version which played to packed houses at Portishead for those two days. The film was a little under 30 minutes in length.

The War was taking its toll in 1916 and the Assembly Hall was requisitioned by the Army in October of that year. The following announcement appeared in the *Clevedon Mercury*.

The Management very much regret to inform their numerous patrons that, owing to the action of the Military authorities in commandeering their Hall, the advertised programme will not be run this week. The Management are considering the possibilities of securing a temporary arrangement which will enable them to carry on the serial picture now running, but at times like these it must be understood that there are many difficulties to contend with. However, it is hoped that some way may be found to continue the only amusement in Portishead, and our patrons may rest assured that if our efforts come to naught, it will not be the fault of the Management.

This was in the issue dated 14 October and the serial concerned 'Broken Coin' (1915) starring Grace Cunard which was running at the time and with the seventh episode about to run the serial was less than half way through the 15 episodes. It was under consideration that to complete the serial it would be shown along with other films in Pierrot's Pavilion in the Esplanade Gardens (now the Lake Grounds). Because of some technical problems but mainly opposition to the plan by Bristol Corporation, in those days having many rights over land in Portishead, the proposal fell through.

Scenes from the serial "Broken Coin" (1915) which when shown at the cinema was itself 'broken' due to War requirements placed on the use of the Assembly Hall. *Authors collection*

Eventually the Military reconsidered and permitted the Hall to operate as a cinema again after a lapse of two months and it re-opened for pictures on Thursday 14 December with a good programme which saw the continuance of the serial 'Broken Coin'.

It would have been interesting to know if they re-ran the first six episodes again or just started from episode seven.

Scenes from the ever popular "Perils of Pauline" (1914) which was showing to packed houses in 1917. *Authors collection*

Business seems to be good with larger publicity for the cinema with this advertisement in the Clevedon Mercury in 1920. *Courtesy Clevedon Mercury*

Before the re-opening some improvements were made to the Hall notably to the re-seating by installing new tip-up seats. Other notable events which took place in the Assembly Hall cinema included the run of the famous serial 'Perils of Pauline' (1914) some three years after its release. A review in the Clevedon Mercury dated 17 February 1917 said of the serial:

'Perils of Pauline' with Pearl White , Pathe's feerless, peerless girl, plays the part of Pauline in a film of thrilling adventure and daring exploits at the Portishead Cinema on Thursday and Saturday next. The heroine survives many plots to destroy her by means of poisoning, imprisoning in a submarine etc. With all these and more adventures does the daring young heroine pull through?. See for yourself each episode as it appears at the Portishead Picture House commencing Thursday February 22nd at 6.30 pm

The reference to 'Portishead Picture House' is interesting as it was never known as the Picture House. Some confusion with the Clevedon cinema I suspect.

Athough it seems that the cinema was well established in the Assembly Hall Thursdays and Saturdays other entertainment took place on other days. Two notable ones were the appearance of Ernest Bevin on a Sunday afternoon in December 1917 to give a lecture to a full house of 250, mainly dock workers about 'Labour and Government'. He was at that time organiser of the Dockers' Union. An interesting event also took place in May 1919 when a Black and White Minstrel show was staged in the Hall by members of the original Portishead Minstrel Troupe. They had produced shows some twenty-five years previous and by taking on some new members they revived the Minstrel show in aid of the fund for returning local servicemen. The event was very successful raising a lot of money for the Fund. Minstrel shows had been well received in the past and this revival was much applauded. Such an event could not happen these days of course.

Cinema at the Assembly Hall continued much the same throughout the following years. In February 1921 there was need to scotch a rumour that Mr F.J.H. Holme was no longer connected with the Portishead Cinema. Holme was a Director and Secretary of the Company. As no records can be found without going back through the years of Company it must be assumed that by this time the Portishead Cinema was an established Company either renting the Assembly Hall for cinema shows or contracted to do so by the Assembly Hall governing body. What appears to have caused the rumour was that a Mr W.J. Rolph had taken over as Superintendent of the Assembly Hall. At this time also it appears that the Directors of the cinema had taken on new staff.

The Hall had again received some improvements and decoration and it was advertised as being available for concerts on Tuesdays and Fridays. This seems to have been short lived because on and after 19 September 1921 the Portishead cinema was advertised as being open nightly, Monday to Friday at 7 pm and Saturday with performances at 2.30 pm, 6.15 pm and 8.35 pm The film for the new opening times was 'The Elusive Pimpernel' (1919) a film of the Baroness Orchy novel in seven parts.

Seat prices were by this time 6d. 9d. and 1/-. Children were two-and-a-half pence and 4d. for matinees only. By 1923 the prices were 6d., 9d. and 1/3d Children again half price for matinees only. In the winter of 1923 the cinema closed down. The reason for the closure is obscure as it seems not to have been reported. The only indication that it did so was an item in the *Mercury* which appeared in a local news column in September 1924 as follows:

THE CINEMA HALL – One hears constantly reiterated expressions of regret at the closing down last winter of the local cinema, and a hope that it will be opened again. A certain number of residents feel the loss of it particularly and complain of the deadly monotony of life in Portishead during the winter months. The feeling is that the cinema would not be a paying proposition if it opened again for six nights in the week, but that if it could be used for pictures for three nights weekly and let for reasonable terms for other things such as concerts, lectures and meetings, on the other three nights, the hall might be made a remunerative speculation. Will not a few of Portisheads monied people put their heads together and become 'public benefactors' in this direction.

It would seem that some notice was taken. In the latter part of 1923 William Durbin, a wheelwright and carpenter by profession who had premises in the High Street and had an involvement with the cinema operation, took over the role of getting it open again. Based on the suggestions made the Assembly Hall was back on pictures from late 1924 for three nights each week with occasional variety shows on other nights. There were also meetings, lectures and concerts. Bill 'Slab' Durbin, as he was known, managed the cinema side of the Hall. Others who assisted are thought to have been Albert Bessant, as a re-wind boy, and a Mr Dickenson along with Bill Durbin, as projection staff.

There is reference to Bill Durbin joining forces with a Mr Donne in 1927 as partners in the business. This unfortunately cannot be substantiated. Mr Donne, of whom little is known, was by all accounts, running film shows in Clevedon and Nailsea. Unfortunately this also is obscure because the only reported cinema shows of entertainment films in Clevedon took place at the Picture House. I cannot imagine Victor Cox putting up with any opposition. As far as Nailsea is

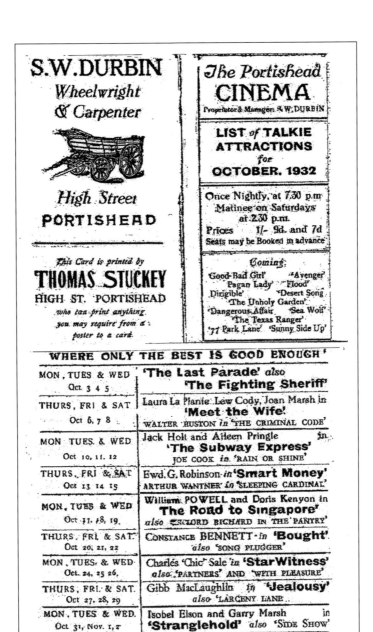

S.W. DURBIN
Wheelwright & Carpenter

High Street
PORTISHEAD

This Card is printed by
THOMAS STUCKEY
HIGH ST. PORTISHEAD
who can print anything
you may require from a
poster to a card.

The Portishead
CINEMA
Proprietor & Manager S.W. DURBIN

**LIST of TALKIE
ATTRACTIONS
for
OCTOBER. 1932**

Once Nightly, at 7.30 p.m
Matinee on Saturdays
at 2.30 p.m.
Prices   1/- 9d. and 7d
Seats may be Booked in advance

Coming
'Good-Bad Girl'   'Avenger'
'Pagan Lady'   'Flood'
'Dirigible'   'Desert Song
'The Unholy Garden'
'Dangerous Affair   'Sea Wolf'
'The Texas Ranger'
'77 Park Lane'   'Sunny Side Up'

'WHERE ONLY THE BEST IS GOOD ENOUGH'

MON, TUES & WED Oct. 3 4 5	**'The Last Parade!'** *also* **'The Fighting Sheriff'**
THURS, FRI & SAT Oct 6, 7 8	Laura La Plante Lew Cody, Joan Marsh in **'Meet the Wife!'** WALTER HUSTON in 'THE CRIMINAL CODE'
MON TUES & WED Oct 10, 11. 12	Jack Holt and Aileen Pringle in **'The Subway Express'** JOE COOK in 'RAIN OR SHINE'
THURS, FRI & SAT Oct 13 14 15	Ewd. G. Robinson in **'Smart Money'** ARTHUR WANTNER in 'SLEEPING CARDINAL'
MON, TUES & WED Oct 17. 18, 19.	William POWELL and Doris Kenyon in **The Road to Singapore'** *also* LORD RICHARD IN THE 'PANTRY'
THURS, FRI & SAT Oct 20, 21, 22	CONSTANCE BENNETT in **'Bought'** *also* 'SONG PLUGGER'
MON, TUES, & WED Oct. 24, 25 26,	Charles 'Chic' Sale in **'Star Witness'** *also* 'PARTNERS' AND 'WITH PLEASURE'
THURS, FRI, & SAT Oct 27, 28, 29	Gibb MacLaughlin in **'Jealousy'** *also* 'LARCENY LANE'
MON, TUES & WED. Oct 31, Nov. 1, 2	Isobel Elson and Garry Marsh in **'Stranglehold'** *also* 'SIDE SHOW'

SEE AND HEAR THE WORLD'S BEST TALKIES

Although poor in quality, it being from a
photo-copy, this is possibly the first month
of operation of the 'new' Portishead Cinema.

This is thought to be a programme of the first month of operation of the new Portishead Cinema in 1932.

concerned no records have been found. Mr Donne may have worked for a time in the projection room at the Picture House, Clevedon but there is nothing to verify that either.

In addition to regular weekly films Bill Durbin was involved in staging other entertainment. For a while the Hall was home to The Portishead Players performances and the Portishead Library Debating Society held regular meetings there. A special lecture recital to celebrate the work of Fredrick Eric Weatherley, the celebrated composer, lyricist and Barrister, was held in October 1926. His music was performed with Mrs Alex Ransom (mezzo-soprano) Mr Edmund Davies (bass) and Mr Frank Halliday (tenor) with Mr Alex Ransom at the piano. Quite what the occasion for the concert is not clear but a similar concert was repeated in 1928.

Regrettably no references to who played the piano accompanying the films exists and it can only be supposed that there were a few local musicians who would take that honoured (or hazardous) role throughout the years of silent pictures. One may well have been Mr Alex Ransom who accompanied concerts during the late 1920s.

The cinema continued in the Assembly Hall and run by Bill Durbin in a similar way until it was taken over entirely by him in 1932.

Technical

Unfortunately there is no record available whatsoever of the projection equipment used over the years in the Assembly Hall. In the early days any make or model of projector available at the time could have been used and likely projected from the floor. After the 1909 Cinematograph Act projectors would have had to be enclosed in a booth and it is likely that one was constructed at the street end of the Hall. In the numerous alterations of the hall room to house the projection equipment was probably built as even for a small outfit as the cinema operation was in the 1920s there would have been twin projectors, change-overs and rewind facilities that would have to have been accommodated also. Looking at the layout for 'talkie' pictures described in the next chapter some idea can be made of similar provision in the Assembly Hall.

At the other end of the Hall was a small but adequate stage with tabs and some lighting.

The screen was in early years a roll-up but in later years a fixed screen was fitted to the back wall. There is no record of a phonograph or similar sound reproducing instrument being installed though likely there was one. Musical accompaniment to silent films was with the piano by the stage.

In the latter years, and because of the impending installation of talkie equipment likely the projectors were any one of makes available at that time and probably second-hand.

THE PORTISHEAD CINEMA.

THURSDAY AND SATURDAY,
AUGUST 31st & SEPTEMBER 2nd.

Exclusive Production,
"VANITY FAIR,"
Founded on Thackeray's Famous Novel,
3,000 feet.

"THE BROKEN COIN," Episode Five,
"THE UNDERGROUND FOE."

"FATTY'S DEBUT,"
A most amusing Keystone Film.

Popular Prices, 4d., 5d., and 7d., including Entertainment Tax.
Children 2d. and 3d. to Matinée only, including Tax.

Local paper advert for the cinema programme for the three days for August 1916

A scene from 'Sign of the Cross' (1915) shown at the Assembly Hall cinema in 1916. *Authors collection*

3. Portishead Cinema

In the early part of the 1930s the Assembly Hall underwent a significant change. Since 1928 'talkies' had come in and the death knell for silent films had sounded. By 1930 few were being made, except for one or two film makers, Chaplin being one, all the studios were now producing sound pictures.

The cinema operation in the Assembly Hall was silent having no sound equipment installed thus unless such equipment was brought in this would mean the end of pictures at the Hall. Additionally of course there was a crisis looming because there was a lack of new silent product and the distributors were terminating silent film releases. By 1932 the situation had become critical.

A new company was formed by Bill Durbin and associates, Cinema (Portishead) Ltd. who took over the Assembly Hall and converted it into a cinema. The conversion was considerable, little of the interior escaping alteration. The projection room was reconstructed to take the sound equipment. A new screen which measured 15 ft by 12 ft was erected on the stage with the speaker system behind . This considerably reduced the depth of the stage which, as remembered from the 1940s, had no tabs.

As to whether there was a raked floor created or not seems to rely on people's memories for some say that it was sloping and others not.

The cinema had 250 seats. From the front the first rows of seats were khaki coloured tip-up type. The remainder were red plush styled seats. The projection room did not stretch the full width of the cinema which left an alcove. Here the highest priced seats were installed again with red plush and with a higher level of comfort. There were two aisles and one across the screen end with another adjacent to the projection room.

The entrance was where it is situated today and as you entered there was a small foyer where the pay desk and confectionery stall were accommodated. Passing through double doors, situated as they still are in the building, led you into the auditorium. Toilets were off to the right of the auditorium and each side of the stage were exit doors leading to exit ways and other rooms. In earlier times the Assembly Hall rear exits led out into a courtyard where the stables for Hunt's horse and carriage business in The Cabstand had stood. The conversion retained these exits which by then led out to the Clockhouse Garage site at the rear of the cinema. Today all of this has been swept away and replaced by housing. The court yard still exists and takes its name from the days when the garage existed and the cinema was operating.

The Portishead Cinema's war effort. The picture shows children involved in a Second World War waste paper collection. William Durbin is on the left and the other gentleman is thought to be an 'official' of the scheme. *Courtesy of Kenneth Crowhurst*

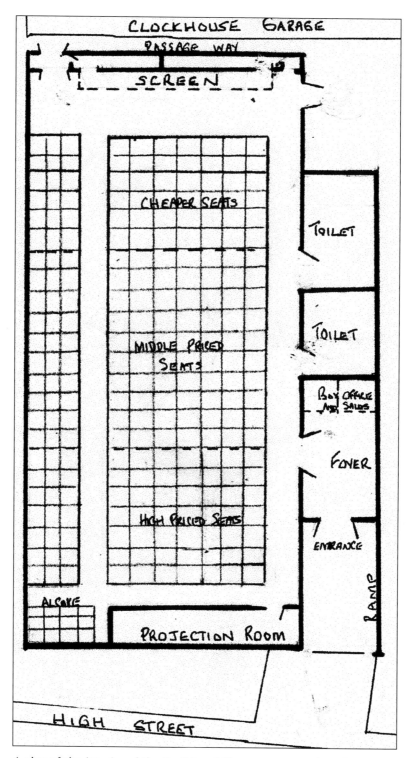

A plan of the interior of the Portishead Cinema as remembered in the
1940's by A. Poole

Just about the most irritating obstacle to showing pictures in the building must have been the Lantern roof. How this was overcome is not recorded during the days of silent shows. There must have been some method of closing off the roof light when pictures were shown and it is expected that some sort of shuttering or blinds were employed. When the hall was converted into a cinema flaps were installed which were operated by ropes and pulleys and the lantern roof was closed off prior to performances. Lighting in the auditorium consisted of decorative suspended lamps and wall lamps which were used as secondary lighting for emergencies. The little cinema was quite cosy even if its décor was nondescript. Simply called the 'Cinema' the only signage on the exterior was a painted board across the entrance to the slope up to the doors. (see picture) and a publicity display at the foot. Neon lighting for the Portishead Cinema was never likely to have been installed.

The Cinema opened as far as can be ascertained on the 3 October 1932 with a grand action double bill programme including 'The Last Parade' (1931) starring Jack Holt and Constance Cummings. The film was a character melodrama. The second feature was a typical 'B' rip-roaring western escapade called 'The Fighting Sheriff' For the second half of that first week, Thursday to Saturday Laura LaPlante, Lew Cody and Joan Marsh starred in 'Meet The Wife' (1931) an romantic comedy. Miss LaPlante had her first talking role in 'Showboat' (1929) and Lew Cody, also a star from silent days and had crossed over successfully to the talkies. He was French and was in great demand in the early sound days because of his accent. The second feature was 'The Criminal Code' (1931) with Walter Huston. Aficionado film-goers might better remember him for his endearing performance in 'Treasure of the Sierra Madre' (1947).

The new cinema became an immediate success the patrons taking an instant liking to the talkies. Seat prices at this time were 7d., 9d. and 1/- for the better and double seats that were in the alcove. Performances were nightly (except Sundays) at 7.30 pm with a matinee on Saturdays at 2.30 pm There was an advanced ticket purchase arrangement which was very popular especially for Saturday evenings. The publicity announced that the Cinema was 'where only the best is good enough' and 'see and hear the world's best talkies'. Perhaps a little pretentious for such a small operation but it at least showed the will to make the business a success which was to continue for the next twenty years or so.

Children were catered for with a matinee on Saturday afternoon which would be the same programme as the evening. The prices were 3d. and 4d. The policy of adult pricing for children at evening shows was continued from the silent days.

One innovative piece of programming was the running of serials in the early evening for children, usually on Tuesday or Friday soon after school hours. These continued for many years. Alfred Poole remembers them quite clearly. His encounter with Flash Gordon came around 1937 when having attended one of the after schools shows he became too frightened to walk home in the dark. By the early 1940s the children's shows had moved to Saturday morning with special programming.

In common with all cinemas in the country the Cinema closed for a few days at the start of the Second World War but it was soon open again when the restrictions were lifted and like all cinemas of the period business was brisk particularly with the incoming of the armed services to the area. The build up to D-day in 1944 was particularly evident in Portishead docks which brought extra trade to the little cinema in the High Street. Whilst there were frequent air raids over the area the cinema was spared and legend has it that the shows were never interrupted the patrons choosing to stay or leave as they wished if the warning sounded.

In June 1946 it was announced that Bill Durbin was retire as proprietor of Portishead Cinema Ltd. after 23 years of operating it. Upon retirement he sold the business to a private company. According to the Kinematograph Year Book for 1947 the new owner was L.F. Davies, of Scotland House, Coombe Road, Portishead although a couple of years later it gave the address as Foxholes Cottage, Exmouth. The year books, as I mention in the Clevedon writings, depended solely upon cinemas up-dating the information about themselves so as to the authenticity of entries at any given time can be suspect. Management of the cinema was taken on by Edward Phelan who was Bill Durbin's son-in-law and he had worked with Bill in both a projection and management capacity for eleven years.

The cinema went on to continuous performances from 6 pm daily except Sunday. As far as can be ascertained there were never any performances on a Sunday though from time to time a concert was arranged. Seat prices up to the time of the sale were 10d. and 1/2d. The more expensive seats were raised to 2/- by the new owner. The seating capacity was reduced to 200. Just about a year later the cinema underwent a minor refurbishment and the seating was further reduced to 165. There was also a price increase to 1/- for the ordinary seats and 2/5d. for the more comfortable seats in the alcove (the odd pence prices were caused by the entertainment tax levied in those days).

People who are recorded as working at the Cinema during the period it was on talkies with both Bill Durbin and Ted Phelan include Miss E. Curtis who was cashier in 1945. She was also later listed as the Licensee and Manageress. Albert

The old cinema building as seen today and now the Library. Little seems to have changed with the exterior.

A rear view of the old cinema building and it has changed little.

Another view of the building this time providing a view of the Lantern roof.

Bessant and Fred Small were projectionists though a Mr Wood and Mr Dickson are also listed as projectionists. Ida Phelan, wife of Ted Phelan, also worked at the cinema from time to time.

The Portishead Cinema was most definitely a popular venue for the people of Portishead during those years. It never seemed to have shown the latest releases and played the programmes that kept its audiences happy. Most of the programmes right up to the last were double feature shows, the second feature being a 'B' picture. There is no record of regular newsreels having been shown there though during the Second World War there must have been. Some of the titles that comprised the programmes reflect the type of film fare offered during the 1940s :

'The Gaunt Stranger' (1938) with Wilfred Lawson
        plus 'The Great White Trail'

'Look Up and Laugh' (1935) with Gracie Fields (her sixth film for Basil Dean)
        plus 'Tarzan Trailing Trouble' with Bill Maynard as Tarzan

'Its In The Air' (1938) starring the ever popular George Formby
        plus Tex Ritter in Texas Country (1937).

and two from the 1950s:

'Only The Valiant' (1950) starring Gregory Peck and Barbara Peyton
        plus 'East Of The River' (1940) with John Garfield

and a rare showing of a musical:

'Brigadoon' (1954) starring Gene Kelly and Cyd Charisse
        plus 'Brewsters Millions' (1935) with Jack Buchanon

Two good double bills which should have brought in good business.

So the little cinema was still plodding along with its policy of pleasing its regular patrons twice weekly well into the days of television and still doing quite good business. A few of the more spectacular Hollywood epics must have played there from time to time even if it was years after everyone had seen them. Probably the most prestigious film to have reached the Portishead screen was soon after the Coronation of Queen Elizabeth II. When 'A Queen Is Crowned'(1953) was shown to packed houses and this time there was no second feature.

Monday, November 1st. For Three Days
Victor Mature and Jean Simmons in
AFFAIR WITH A STRANGER Ⓤ 6-0, 8-40
Also Tim Holt in **Storm Over Wyoming** Ⓤ
7-30

Thursday, November 4th. For Three Days
Alan Ladd and Leo Genn in
THE RED BERET Ⓤ Technicolor 6-0, 8-40
Also Gene Autry in **Blue Canadian Rockies**
7-30 Ⓤ

Monday, November 8th. For Three Days
Gregory Peck and Barbara Payton in
ONLY THE VALIANT Ⓐ 6-0, 9-5
Also John Garfield and Brenda Marshall in
East of the River Ⓐ 7-45

Thursday, November 11th. For Three Days
John Bentley and Patricia Dainton in
HAMMER THE TOFF Ⓤ 6-10, 8-40
Eddie Dean in **Check Your Guns** Ⓤ 7-25

Monday, November 15th. For Three Days
James Cagney and Phyllis Thaxter in
COME FILL THE CUP Ⓐ 6-0, 9-0
Also Ronald Reagan and Roselle Towne in
Code of the Secret Service Ⓐ 7-50

Thursday, Nov. 18th. For Three Days
Joan Collins and George Cole in
OUR GIRL FRIDAY Ⓤ Glorious Colour
6-0 and 8-40
Also Eddie Dean and His Horse "Copper" in
The Westward Trail Ⓤ 7-30

Monday, Nov. 22nd. For Three Days
Patricia Medina and John Sands in
ALADDIN AND HIS LAMP Ⓤ Cinecolor
6-10 and 8-35
Also Leo Gorcey and The Bowery Boys in
Feudin' Fools Ⓤ 7-20

Thursday, Nov. 25th. For Three Days
George Montgomery and Tab Hunter in
GUN BELT Ⓤ In Technicolor 6-10, 8-40
Also Mikel Conrad and Doris Merrick in
Untamed Women Ⓤ 7-25

Monday, Nov. 29th. For Three Days
Mickey Rooney and Dick Haymes in
ALL ASHORE Ⓤ In Technicolor 6-0, 8-50
Also Bonar Colleano and Mary Castle in
Eight Iron Men Ⓐ 7-20

A programme for the month of November 1954. A little over a a year later the cinema closed.

By the mid 1950s the writing was on the wall for the cinema. Colour TV was with us and the without ability to attract sufficient customers left the cinema proprietors with little to spend on the new cinema technology that was revolutionising the industry. With Cinemascope sweeping the country's cinemas those halls which were to small to convert to the wide screen were shutting down or turning to Bingo. Sadly the Portishead Cinema was one of these and on Saturday 31 December 1955 it closed. The last film was 'The Far Country' (1954) starring James Stewart, Walter Brennan and Ruth Roman. It was a sturdy Western with three leading stars of the day and it was a fitting film to end twenty-three years of the rip roaring talkies that the cinema specialised in.

An entry in the 'Mercury' on that Saturday reported:

Portishead Cinema is closing tonight and when the last performance is over the staff will go home with a glorious vista of free evenings ahead. For Miss E. Curtis, who has sat in the booking office for something like 39years, it will be a change indeed. She started working in the silent days when the atmosphere was created by a piano.

So the little cinema with humble beginnings that never amounted to much in the glittering world of the super cinemas closed its doors forever with the knowledge that in its short life it had provided a way of life and enjoyment for many and at last has been recorded for posterity.

Note: The Portishead Library was at that time in Falcondale Road. After the necessary alterations to the old cinema the Library moved into it which made room for the Youth Club. The Library is still there today.

Technical

With the installation of sound equipment in 1932 we can only rely upon the Kinematograph Year books to provide any details of the projection equipment and very few people who have recollections about the early days.

The first 'talkie' installation was an Edibell Sound System and said to have high quality photo-sound reproduction. By 1940 the sound system had changed to a Morrison and in 1942 to a Gyrotone system. By the 1950s it was reported to be Western Electric.

The conversion was too late to have seen Vitaphone sound-on-disk equipment installed.

As to the projectors. There is no information that I have been able to secure which indicates the projection heads but like most small cinemas of its type they were possibly Kalee 7's or 8's, in the beginning changing to later Kalee models by the fifties.

It is also known that Gaumont Kalee equipment was installed as early as 1920 with established knowledge that when the projection equipment was up-dated for showing of 'talkies' Gaumont-Kalee equipment was installed.

Mr Fred Small

For many years after the closure of the cinema, films were still shown in Portishead.

Fred Small had worked as a projectionist at the Cinema for many years. He also was an ice cream vendor and postman in the town. After the cinema closed he ran a mobile cinema operation every week during the winter season for many years. Setting up in the Folk Hall and later in the Somerset Hall he provided filmed entertainment using 16 mm.

The release of 16 mm films were usually twelve months after the 35 mm cinema release and Fred was able to keep his patrons fairly well up to date with films. Moderately priced the shows were well attended by and large. His operation took him outside of the town also with shows at the Cadbury Country Club at Yatton and shows at nearby Pill. I think he closed down in the late 1980s. The cost of hiring the films had increased considerably in the latter years and that was probably the reason Fred Small gave up.

Although mobile operator Fred continued the pleasure of film-going for many people in Portishead for a number of years after the cinema had closed and deserves the celebration of cinema with which this book is concerned.

4. Conclusion

Portishead Cinema is a prime example of the many cinemas that could be found in small towns in the rural areas of Great Britain. They were almost without exception conversions from other uses such as village halls, chapels and the like . Some others were purpose built to fine architectural trends of the time and high standards of comfort, others not so. Regardless of how they looked they fulfilled a need and probably never so effectively than during the 'golden years' when going to the pictures meant a good night of entertainment which could last for three hours or more and particularly during the years of War.

Many were classed as 'flea-pits' but were they really? The two cinemas featured in this book about motion-picture entertainment in far North Somerset in the main were above such description though both suffered that inglorious description at times. Both cinemas were created the by the efforts of local entrepreneurs and both were successful in their own way, one of the cinemas still with us today.

Portishead is without a cinema now although the Curzon at Clevedon is regarded by some Portishead residents as their local cinema. It seems, by a letter written to the local paper in 1992, that a call was being made to seek a cinema operation in the Folk Hall. This was in response to the loss of the mobile operation run by Fred Small, which had ceased I suspect. Similar views have been expressed from time to time. It would appear there is still a feeling for such a venture for the town. Whether in the future cinema will be revived in or near to Portishead cannot be foretold. There is a tremendous amount of re-development going on with the Marina, hundreds and hundreds of houses planned with the attendant services and facilities but very little of this includes entertainment. Perhaps someday a cinema concern might see the opening of a small multiplex in the locality a profitable proposition?. Portishead is expected to have a population of nearly 30.000 making it the biggest town, bar Weston-super-Mare, in North Somerset and add to that the populations of nearby towns, even Clevedon, it might look promising for some developer and operator.

Whilst Portishead cannot subscribe to having had an 'everlasting picture show' it is important that its little cinema be remembered and its existence recorded for posterity and for that reason alone deserves inclusion in this celebration of local cinema.

The End

Acknowledgements

There are many without whose help I could not have written this book and to whom I am deeply grateful. Space permits me to only mention a few but to everyone who has supported me in this endeavour a sincere thankyou.

D. Bishop, A. Blackmore, The late Joan Birch, R. & L. Butland, Barbara Connel, Aubrey Cook, Kenneth S. Crowhurst, R. Deerburgh, G. Dimond, B. Dixon, Carol Deacon, V. Olver, S. Drew, Jim and Mary Dyer, Mr & Mrs H. Edwards, B. Goodsall, S. Herbert – Projected Picture Trust, Margaret Keeley, P. Leverett, Jane Lilly, Jeanette Maycock, Bert Price, A.Poole, Paul Scott, Jon Webber, C. Preece & J. Reagan (USA), Alan Smart – Projected Picture Trust Canada, The late Graeham Whitehead-Ashorn Hall, Warwickshire. Colleagues at the Curzon Cinema.

Organisations

Bristol City Council, The British Film Institute, Cinema Theatres Association, Clevedon Civic Society, 'Clevedon Mercury', Clevedon Newspapers Ltd., Country Gardens, Clevedon, The Imperial War Museum, North Somerset Library Service – Clevedon and Portishead, Curzon Community Centre for the Arts, Curzon Community Cinema Ltd.

Bibliology

'Travelling Fairs' David Braithwaite. Shire Publishing
'Encyclopedia of British Film' Brian MacFarlane (2003) Methuen
'A History Of Narrative Film' David A. Cook. Norton & Co.
'British Film Year Book –1946 Peter Noble
'Talking Pictures' Bernard Brown (1932)
'Annals of Clevedon' Clevedon Civic Society
'Movies In The West' Richard Lewis (1971)
'A Pictorial History of Silent Cinema', 'A Pictorial History of the Talkies' David Blum.

Acknowledgement for the images used in this book are given with each caption however every effort has been made to locate the origins of images. Please therefore accept apologies where there are errors or omissions.

Design and Layout Geoffrey Blake

Glossary

Throughout the book I have used some terms which might not be familiar with the reader. A Glossary is compiled to assist.

Academy Ratio or aperture

The 'size' of the aperture in the projection gate and picture seen on the screen. Academy ratio was the normal standard picture on cinema screens from 1932, when it was standardized in 1932 until the 1950s.

It had been used as early as the 1890s. Known in the trade as 4 × 3 or 1.33:1. The normal TV screen is 4 × 3. The wide screen is approx: 1:85 to 1 (16 × 9).

Animated Pictures

The name given to the first motion-pictures (also called 'living pictures') taken from the description 'to give life to' 'endowed with life' or 'to give spirit to'. Animated pictures today generally refers to cartoon work and computer graphic art.

Ambient Speakers

Speakers that send the sound 'around' to provide atmosphere to the screen sound. Usually found around the walls of the auditorium.

Bioscope

A cinematograph projector.
A name given to a place where cinematograph films were shown usually on fairgrounds. A travelling Bioscope show. An early cinema.

Cinemascope

Film projection on a wide screen brought into commercial use by Twentieth –Century Fox in 1953. It offered a new ratio of 2.55:1 originally but reduced to 2.35:1 later. It offered an 8 × 3 picture size (roughly twice as wide as high) which in slightly different form is still used today better known as Panavision. Still described in the trade as 'Scope it is only attainable on a cinema screen.

Cine-Variety

Stage acts within the Cinema programme. Very popular during the twenties, thirties and forties when short variety shows were slotted into the film programme. Became popular again for a short time in the sixties when rock & roll bands would 'try out'.

Distributor

The organisation to which the film generally belongs and arranges the bookings for the country's cinemas. Bookings are made with the distributor usually after a 'trade' exhibition of the new film. Distributors have a near monopoly as to who can show their films and are quite strict about the conditions under which the product is shown.

Double-Bill

A film programme with two features. Up until the mid 20th Century they were a staple part of most cinemas. The main feature would be recent release of new or second run film. The second feature would usually be a 'B' picture, cheapies made by the studios to bring on potential stars and directors etc. Double-feature programmes would be two 'main' features.

Exhibitor

Cinema owner/circuit who operate cinemas.

Float

Collective name for lights on a stage. Floats or battens are usually used to illuminate the stage or drapery from above.

Fly/Fly Grid

The area above the stage where the scenery and drop tabs are controlled and 'tied off'. The area where the ropes and machinery is located is called the Fly Grid. Only the larger cinemas had fly towers. Most others would use tabs and drapes such as legs and borders to decorate the stage operated either from side stage or the projection room.

Gas Engine (or Petrol Engine)

Early name for an engine employed specifically to drive a dynamo or generator to provide electricity.

Hall

Used to describe a cinema auditorium or the public seating area of a cinema.

House

Used to describe a cinema auditorium . Describes the state of the attendance i.e. Full-House. Performances such as first house, second house. Category of cinema according to its importance the prestigious ones were AA, the ones generally circuit houses were A.

B were the lesser cinemas as C the lower of the classification. The Clevedon cinema was a C for most of its life.

Kinematograph
Another name for cinematograph.

LH. Centre. RH Channels and Speakers
The channels on the film soundtrack carrying the sound to where the actors/sounds appear on the screen. The speakers receiving those channels set at the appropriate positions behind the screen enabling the sound to come from the correct regions on the screen. Effects are usually directed to the ambient speakers around the auditorium.

Light Source
System for providing the light for motion-picture projection. In the early days oil, gas, limelight. Later carbon arc lamps were used and today the illumination for film projection is a Xenon lamp.

Myrioama
A stage entertainment of Victorian and Edwardian times which consisted of a series of tableaux depicting historical and patriotic scenes. Music and speech accompanied the scenes to which later was augmented by the use of the cinematograph.

National release.
The date when a film is first released for general exhibition.

Phonograph.
Basically a recording on a cylinder operated mechanically to reproduce sound through a horn or similar. (derives from Edison's instrument). Used before the platter system or disk was perfected and became known as the Gramophone.

Photophone.
A synchronisedd sound alongside film system marrying picture and sound indelibly together. Known as sound-on-film. The name mainly the preserve of the Radio Corporation of America (RCA) Known as optical sound in the trade.

Proscenium

The front part of the stage. The stage opening. The surround is known as the proscenium arch. Found in most traditional theatres and cinemas. Now superseded by wall-to-wall screens.

Rake

The slope of an auditorium floor so that the seating is arranged permitting sight of the screen without obstruction. The Picture House (Curzon) rake is severe due to building over the original cinema. Modern auditoriums are usually designed with stadium seating for comfortable viewing of the screen as well as some 'raking' Term also can refer to the angle of a projector or screen.

Roxy-box

A large cabinet housing a number of speakers usually behind the screen. Originate from the early 'talkie' days and still found in some cinemas in later times. Usually a large horn speaker arrangement could be found installed on the top of the Roxy-box.

Split-week

Division of the week into separate programmes playing from Monday to Wednesday with a change for Thursday to Saturday. This was profitable for small cinemas who would not have been able to sustain a full week on one film. Some cinemas divided the week into three programmes Mon/Tues, Wed/Thurs and Fri.Sat. That was known as a triple split used by some owners with three cinemas in towns of close proximity.

Screen Talk and Audio Description

A system whereby a sub-title is screened on the film for the aid of patrons who have hearing difficulties. Audio Description provides for patrons with sight difficulties and gives a 'running commentary' of the action taking place on the screen. It is controlled from the projection room using the latest sound reproduction and electronic projection.

Tabs

Stage Curtains. The ones immediately behind the proscenium are front tabs and those covering the screen are Screen Tabs. In the more lavish cinemas there were festoon tabs which were drop curtains.

Vitaphone

A Sound-on-Disk system developed to provide music to silent pictures originally but developed to provide 'talking pictures' in 1926/27 and lasted until around 1931.

Vivaphone

A sound-on-disk system perfected by Cecil Hepworth, a British pioneer, which used at first a wax cylinder phonograph to reproduce sound to pictures and then later a disk and gramophone and horn. It was sychronised to the projector by using an intermediate mechanism operated by coloured glasses, ratchets and electro-magnets.

Volaries of Terpiscore

and for those who are puzzled by the quotation in the account of the Assembly Hall at Portishead it can be roughly described as 'dedicated persons being mentally absorbed in the music of choral song and dance'. There you have it.